AD

Architectural Design
July/August 2009

Digital Cities

Guest-edited by Neil Leach

IN THIS ISSUE
Main Section

POWER TO THE PARAMETRIC
Patrik Schumacher of Zaha Hadid Architects, espouses parametricism as the dominant style of today's avant-garde and demonstrates its potential for large-scale urban schemes. P 14

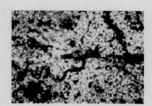

URBAN BREEDER
Could well-adapted urban design be best developed by breeding cities in 'digital laboratories'? **Michael Batty**, Bartlett Professor at UCL, puts his evolutionary ideas to the test. P 46

DIGITAL DELIBERATIONS WITH DELANDA
Well-known 'street philosopher' and professor **Manuel DeLanda** discusses his thoughts on urban simulation in an interview with guest-editor Neil Leach. P 50

AD+

A TRIBUTE TO AN EXTRAORDINARY FRIEND
Ivan Margolius pays homage to the visionary and truly unique creative talent of Czech architect **Jan Kaplický**, who was for many years a loyal friend to *AD*. P 100+

ENCORE!
Jayne Merkel reviews the imaginative remodelling of the interior of Alice Tully Hall, the first space in the Lincoln Center in New York to be renovated by Diller Scofidio + Renfro. P 108+

WILEY
wiley.com

Architectural Design

Vol 79, No 4 (July/August 2009)
ISSN 0003-8504

Profile No 200
ISBN 978-0470 773000

Editorial Offices
John Wiley & Sons
International House
Ealing Broadway Centre
London W5 5DB

T: +44 (0)20 8326 3800

Editor
Helen Castle

Regular columnists: Valentina Croci, David Littlefield, Jayne Merkel, Will McLean, Neil Spiller, Michael Weinstock and Ken Yeang

Freelance Managing Editor
Caroline Ellerby

Production Editor
Elizabeth Gongde

Design and Prepress
Artmedia, London

Printed in Italy by Conti Tipocolor

Sponsorship/advertising
Faith Pidduck/Wayne Frost
T: +44 (0)1243 770254
E: fpidduck@wiley.co.uk

Front cover: Zaha Hadid Architects, Kartal-Penkik masterplan, massing study, Istanbul, Turkey, 2006. © Courtesy Zaha Hadid Architects.

Subscribe to AD

AD is published bimonthly and is available to purchase on both a subscription basis and as individual volumes at the following prices.

PRICES
Individual copies: £22.99/$45.00
Mailing fees may apply

ANNUAL SUBSCRIPTION RATES
Student: UK£70/US$110 print only
Individual: UK £110/US$170 print only
Institutional: UK£180/US$335 print or online
Institutional: UK£198/US$369 combined print and online

Subscription Offices UK
John Wiley & Sons Ltd
Journals Administration Department
1 Oldlands Way, Bognor Regis
West Sussex, PO22 9SA
T: +44 (0)1243 843272
F: +44 (0)1243 843232
E: cs-journals@wiley.co.uk

[ISSN: 0003-8504]

Prices are for six issues and include postage and handling charges. Periodicals postage paid at Jamaica, NY 11431. Air freight and mailing in the USA by Publications Expediting Services Inc, 200 Meacham Avenue, Elmont, NY 11003.
Individual rate subscriptions must be paid by personal cheque or credit card. Individual rate subscriptions may not be resold or used as library copies.

All prices are subject to change without notice.

Postmaster
Send address changes to 3 Publications Expediting Services, 200 Meacham Avenue, Elmont, NY 11003

RIGHTS AND PERMISSIONS
Requests to the Publisher should be addressed to:
Permissions Department
John Wiley & Sons Ltd
The Atrium
Southern Gate
Chichester
West Sussex PO19 8SQ
England

F: +44 (0)1243 770620
E: permreq@wiley.co.uk

CONTENTS

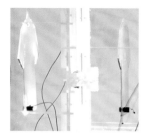

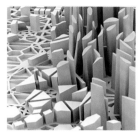

Editorial

Helen Castle

If a house was once a machine for living in can the city now be an iPhone? In this issue of *AD*, LA-based theorist and design strategist Benjamin Bratton posits the idea that the way that we perceive and experience the city has been irreparably shifted by the arrival of the iPhone and similar handheld devices. To some extent the iPhone, with its highly tactile graphic interface and accessible datascapes or 'apps', could even be regarded as usurping some of the key characteristics of the physical metropolis that brings people, goods, markets, communications and information together in one place. The implications here may be far-reaching, but they are very much of the present.

The example of the iPhone suggests just how omnipresent and influential computer technologies have become in the urban realm. It is not, though, entirely indicative of the overarching themes of this issue. As guest-editor Neil Leach articulately explains himself in the opening paragraph of his introduction, the main intention of this title of *AD* is to look at how the digital design tools that have played such a major role in architectural production in the last decade or so might also be shifted up a gear and transferred to urban design. Formally, certain advanced parametric design tools are a strong influence on the aesthetic throughout the issue. This is at its most evident in the masterplans of Zaha Hadid Architects, the Design Research Laboratory (DRL) at the Architectural Association and the digital towers section, which features work by architects and premier architecture schools from around the world. The formal language of the parametric is most strongly advocated by Patrik Schumacher who regards it stylistically as the rightful heir to Modernism. The adoption of digital design tools, however, here play just as an important part for urban analysis as form-finding. Professor Michael Batty, for instance, describes how cities' shapes might be 'grown' in digital laboratories in order to aid evolved urban design.

If the application of digital processes is a consistent theme of the issue, so is the way that it is perceived. Long gone is the Modernist perception that the city is something to be ordered and controlled. Instead, it is regarded as having its own collective intelligence and underlying pattern, as most overtly expressed by Neil Leach's own article on 'swarm intelligence'. The most extreme manifestation of this is François Roche's vision of a habitable organism or biostructure that is responsive to human occupation but develops its own adaptive behaviour. The sense of otherness, which the urban now engenders, combines to make the city ever more intriguing. The urban has never been more irresistible to architects. The city, in all its guises, as demonstrated by this issue, provides an object of endless fascination and seemingly limitless architectural research and analysis. ⟁

Xiaoqin Chen, Runqing Zhang, Ying Liu and Juhi Dhar, Termite Urbanism, MArch, University of Southern California, Los Angeles, 2009
This project attempts to establish an environmentally responsible approach to urban planning using techniques of scripting. Following the principles of traditional wind towers, it employs a 'termite logic' processing script to cut ventilation shafts through the buildings and also employs other forms of scripting in Rhino and processing to generate a coherent urban vision for Dubai.

Introduction

Digital Cities

By Neil Leach

Pavlos Fereos, Konstantinos Grigoriadis, Alexander Robles Palacio and Irene Shamma, Urban Reef, Design Research Lab (DRL), Architectural Association, London, 2009
Urban Reef addresses the problems of localised ground discontinuity and programmatic and physical isolation within a larger urban area by proposing a highly connected 3-D network of housing integrated with commercial and recreational uses for the Hudson's Yard area of New York. Working to a brief for 3,000 housing units, the normative isolated high-rise building type is replaced by a series of mid-rise buildings that incline to minimise structural spans and interconnect in order to maximise the area for housing development.

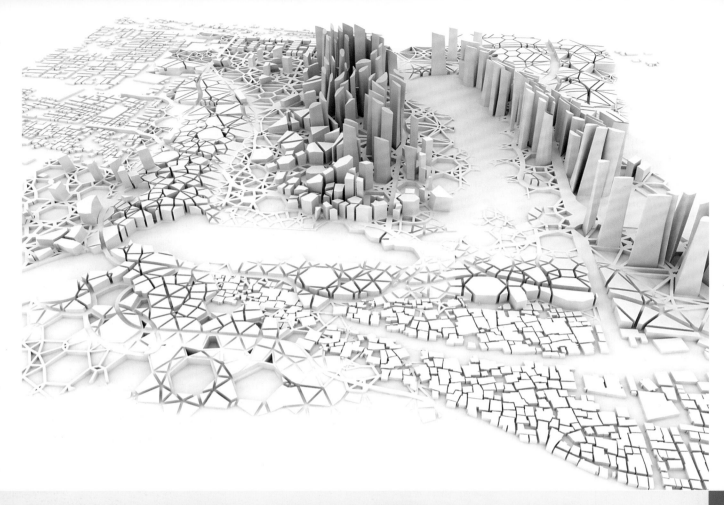

Lindsay Bresser, Claudia Dorner and Sergio Reyes Rodriguez, 123, Design Research Lab (DRL), Architectural Association, London, 2009
123 challenges the proliferation of haphazard urbanisation and incoherent architecture resulting from the accelerated globalisation of the Gulf region via research on the algorithmic and geometric principles inherent in traditional Arabic patterns. This algorithmic approach constitutes the basis for a new scripted morphology generating variation and difference across urban fields, clusters and architectural systems. The proposal aims to create diverse, interactive metropolitan spaces that challenge the generic and disconnected qualities of the current Dubai model by offering flexibility within a repetitive coherence.

For some time now, digital technologies have had a substantial impact on architectural design. From the use of standard drafting packages to the more experimental use of generative design tools, they have come to play a major role in architectural production. But how might these digital technologies help us to design cities? It would seem that we are now entering a new threshold condition, as the application of these tools has begun to shift up a scale to the level of the urban. This issue tracks these developments, and considers the real potential of using these tools not only to design better cities for the future, but also to understand and analyse our existing cities, and navigate them in new ways.

Patrik Schumacher opens the issue with an impassioned plea for 'parametricism' as a new style for architecture and urbanism. Challenging Le Corbusier's celebration of the orthogonal, he argues instead in favour of the parametric, citing the form-finding research of Frei Otto and illustrating his argument with a series of large-scale urban projects by Zaha Hadid Architects.

The theme of parametricism is continued in Tom Verebes' article on the research into urban design undertaken at the Design Research Laboratory (DRL) at the Architectural Association in London. Verebes offers an overview of a series of large-scale urban projects that pursue the design agenda of 'parametric urbanism'.

The work of Hernan Diaz Alonso and François Roche has often been compared, and here the two offer their own idiosyncratic and personal visions of the city of the future, drawing upon a sense of the science-fictional that characterised much of the early exploration into the potential of digital design. Hernan Diaz Alonso's vision is articulated through a visionary movie about the future of Los Angeles. *Chlorofilia* presents a utopian/dystopian vision of a post-apocalyptic LA that has adjusted to the flooding of the city and developed a self-sustaining environment, where cells have become the new bricks and can reform and recombine based on intelligence feedback loops. Roche's vision is equally provocative: 'I've heard

The world of philosophy, it would seem, can still offer incisive insights into the increasingly technological landscape of today.

about …' is a habitable organism – a biostructure – that develops its own adaptive behaviour based on growth scripts, open algorithms and impulses of human occupation. It is built by a construction engine – the Viab – that secretes the landscape through which it moves.

The question then arises as to how these digital tools can be used at a larger scale to generate and model cities. Michael Batty considers the possibility of 'breeding' cities using fractals, cellular automata and so on. But Manuel DeLanda is more cautious in his approach. For him, it is a question of not looking at form itself, but at the decision-making processes that lead to the generation of form. Only then will we be in a position to simulate convincingly the growth of actual cities.

The next two articles pursue the theme of generating urban designs through digital techniques, and draw on the relevance of Gilles Deleuze's thinking to this field. In my own article on 'Swarm Urbanism' I go on to explore the potential of 'swarm intelligence' in urban design, and look at how we can use Deleuze's concept of the 'rhizome'

to better understand the relationships between users and the physical fabric of the city. Peter Trummer then looks at the potential of using associative design principles to model cities in a morphogenetic fashion, articulating his argument through the Deleuzian term, the 'machinic phylum'. The world of philosophy, it would seem, can still offer incisive insights into the increasingly technological landscape of today.

The theme of generating designs is taken further in the section on digital towers, which explores the potential of new digital tools to design architecture at the level of the individual building. The featured towers have been designed by a range of students and practising architects. None has been constructed, but together they offer us an overview of a new approach towards designing large-scale urban buildings harnessing increasingly popular digital techniques.

Such digital tools, though, may also be used to understand and analyse the operations of cities. One of the leading pioneers in using digital tools to model cities and understand the way that they operate has been Space Syntax Ltd. Alain Chiaradia outlines the principles behind the logic of Space Syntax, illustrating them with a study of Tower Hamlets in London.

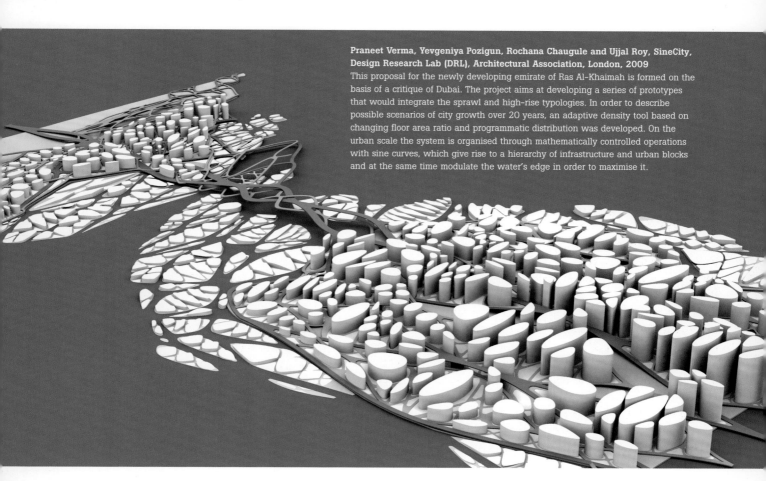

Praneet Verma, Yevgeniya Pozigun, Rochana Chaugule and Ujjal Roy, SineCity, Design Research Lab (DRL), Architectural Association, London, 2009
This proposal for the newly developing emirate of Ras Al-Khaimah is formed on the basis of a critique of Dubai. The project aims at developing a series of prototypes that would integrate the sprawl and high-rise typologies. In order to describe possible scenarios of city growth over 20 years, an adaptive density tool based on changing floor area ratio and programmatic distribution was developed. On the urban scale the system is organised through mathematically controlled operations with sine curves, which give rise to a hierarchy of infrastructure and urban blocks and at the same time modulate the water's edge in order to maximise it.

Britta Knobel, Arnoldo Rabago and Khuzema Hussain, Interconnected Fragmentation, Design Research Lab (DRL), Architectural Association, London, 2006
London has a history of increasing density within defined boundaries. This has always been a space-filling system of politics and economy. The lack of adaptive growth strategies has resulted in a multitude of irregular-shaped voids. Here a new space-filling system is designed to embrace different sites and programmes and to react according to its context. This new technique would follow the logic of a fractal and therefore recursively densify void spaces. As a testing scenario the system was implemented in one of the densest parts of the City of London where there is a real need for more space.

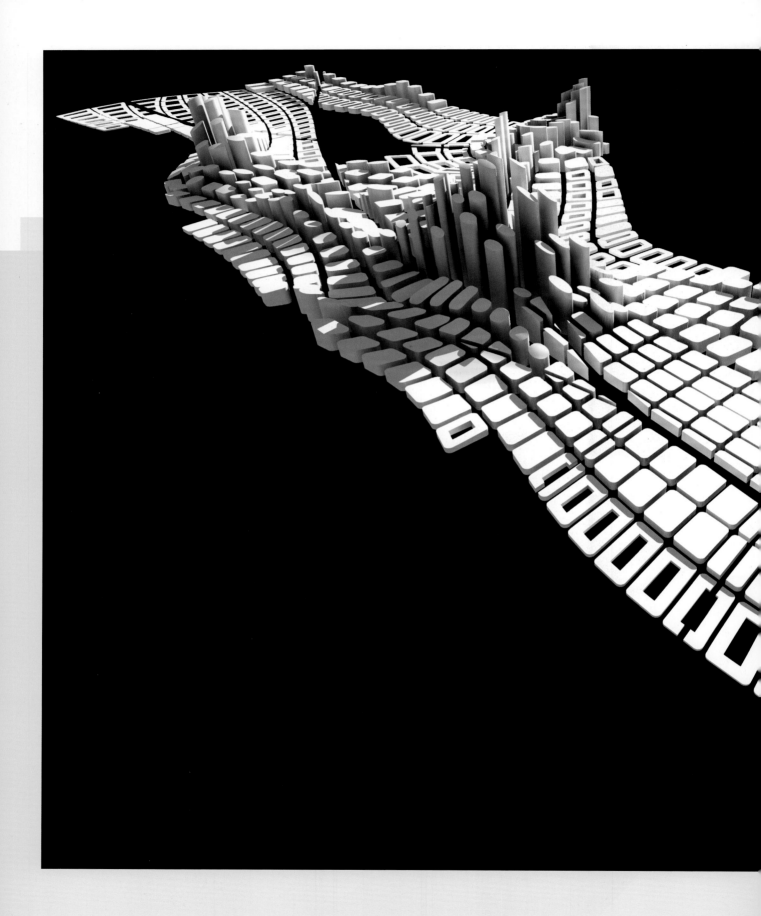

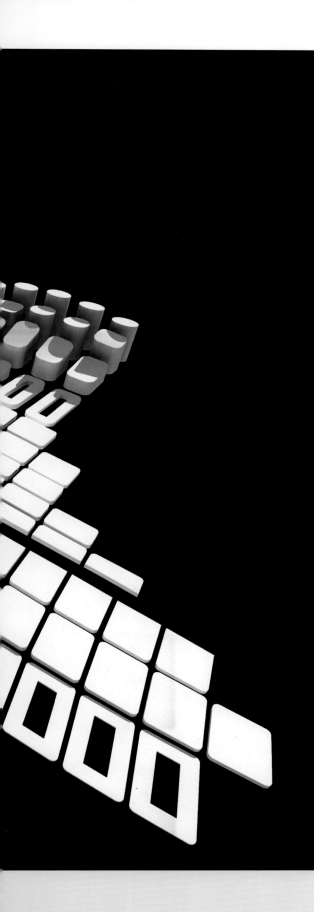

Annie Chan and Yikai Lin, Ant Urbanism, MArch, University of Southern California, Los Angeles, 2009
This project creates a radically new urbanism for an inner-city area of Taipei currently occupied by an airport. Pathways are generated using 'swarm logic' processing techniques based on the principle of the pheromone trails of ants. Rhino scripting and Grasshopper are then used to generate the building themselves.

Equally, the city itself has also been transformed by digital technologies. The contributions in this issue from Vicente Guallart and Benjamin Bratton explore the question of how we are hooked up within a digital information superhighway. Guallart introduces 'Hyperhabitat', an installation that posits the need to reprogram(me) the structures with which we inhabit the world via the introduction of distributed intelligence in the nodes and structures with which we construct buildings and cities. Meanwhile, in his 'iPhone City' article, Bratton explores the potential of the connectivity afforded by global mapping systems, and looks at how they allow us to navigate the city in new and inventive ways.

Together these articles offer an important overview of a certain crucial moment in time when digital technologies began to have a significant impact on the way that we design and think about our cities. Back in 2002 there had been so little engagement with these technologies at an urban scale that Andrew Gillespie was forced to comment: 'We are left to conclude that planners have yet to develop the awareness, let alone the expertise or appropriate policy intervention mechanisms, that would enable them to influence the spatial development of a digital society. Somebody might be "planning" the future digital city – the telecommunications companies perhaps? – but it certainly doesn't seem to be planners!'[1] As the first decade of the 21st century draws to a close, however, there is evidence of a breakthrough. As this issue demonstrates, a number of key architects, planners and theorists have begun to engage with the question of the digital city in a highly insightful way. ᴆ

Note
1. Andrew Gillespie, 'Digital Lifestyles and the Future City', in Neil Leach (ed), *Designing for a Digital World*, John Wiley & Sons Ltd (London), 2002, p 71.

Parametricism

A New Global Style for Architecture and Urban Design

Though parametricism has its roots in the digital animation techniques of the mid-1990s, it has only fully emerged in recent years with the development of advanced parametric design systems. **Patrik Schumacher** explains why parametricism has become the dominant, single style for avant-garde practice today and why it is particularly suited to large-scale urbanism as exemplified by a series of competition-winning masterplans by Zaha Hadid Architects.

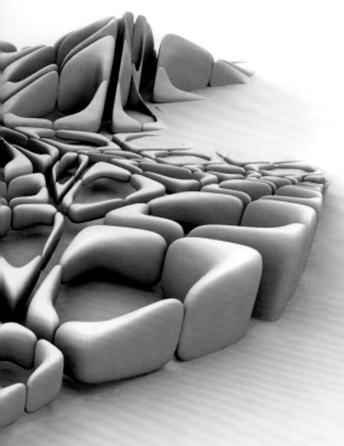

**Zaha Hadid Archiects, Kartal-Pendik
Masterplan, Istanbul, Turkey, 2006**
Fabric study. The urban fabric comprises both
cross towers and perimeter blocks. The image
shows the morphological range of the
perimeter block type. Blocks are split into four
quadrants allowing for a secondary, pedestrian
path system. At certain network crossing
points the block system is assimilated to the
tower system: each block sponsors one of the
quadrants to form a pseudo-tower around a
network crossing point.

There is a global convergence in recent avant-garde architecture that
justifies its designation as a new style: parametricism. It is a style
rooted in digital animation techniques, its latest refinements based on
advanced parametric design systems and scripting methods.
Developed over the past 15 years and now claiming hegemony within
avant-garde architecture practice, it succeeds Modernism as the next
long wave of systematic innovation. Parametricism finally brings to an
end the transitional phase of uncertainty engendered by the crisis of
Modernism and marked by a series of relatively short-lived
architectural episodes that included Postmodernism, Deconstructivism
and Minimalism. So pervasive is the application of its techniques that
parametricism is now evidenced at all scales from architecture to
interior design to large urban design. Indeed, the larger the project, the
more pronounced is parametricism's superior capacity to articulate
programmatic complexity.

The urbanist potential of parametricism has been explored in a
three-year research agenda at the AADRL titled 'Parametric Urbanism'
and is demonstrated by a series of competition-winning masterplans by
Zaha Hadid Architects.

Parametricism as Style
Avant-garde architecture and urbanism are going through a cycle of
innovative adaptation – retooling and refashioning the discipline to
meet the socioeconomic demands of the post-Fordism era. The mass
society that was characterised by a universal consumption standard
has evolved into the heterogeneous society of the multitude, marked by
a proliferation of lifestyles and extensive work-path differentiation. It is
the task of architecture and urbanism to organise and articulate the
increased complexity of our post-Fordist society.

Contemporary avant-garde architecture and urbanism seek to
address this societal demand via a rich panoply of parametric design
techniques. However, what confronts us is a new style rather than
merely a new set of techniques. The techniques in question – the
employment of animation, simulation and form-finding tools, as well as
parametric modelling and scripting – have inspired a new collective
movement with radically new ambitions and values. In turn, this
development has led to many new, systematically connected design
problems that are being worked on competitively by a global network of
design researchers.[1] Over and above aesthetic recognisability, it is this
pervasive, long-term consistency of shared design ambitions/problems
that justifies the enunciation of a new style in the sense of an epochal
phenomenon.[2] Parametricism is a mature style. There has been talk of
'continuous differentiation',[3] versioning, iteration and mass
customisation among other things for quite some time now within
architectural avant-garde discourse.

Not long ago we witnessed an accelerated, cumulative build-up of
virtuosity, resolution and refinement facilitated by the simultaneous
development of parametric design tools and scripts that allow the precise
formulation and execution of intricate correlations between elements
and subsystems. The shared concepts, computational techniques,
formal repertoires and tectonic logics that characterise this work are
crystallising into a solid new hegemonic paradigm for architecture.

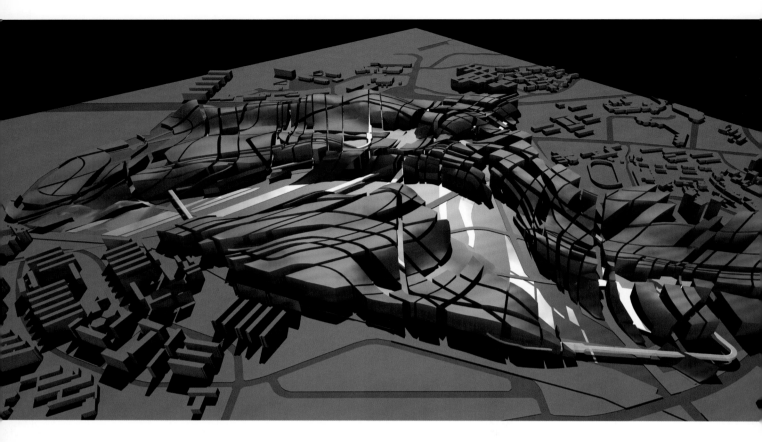

Parametricism emerges from the creative exploitation of parametric design systems in the course of articulating increasingly complex social processes and institutions. That parametric design tools themselves do not account for this profound shift in style from Modernism to parametricism is evidenced by the fact that late Modernist architects are employing parametric tools in ways which result in the maintenance of a Modernist aesthetic, using parametric modelling inconspicuously to absorb complexity. The parametricist sensibility, however, pushes in the opposite direction, aiming for maximum emphasis on conspicuous differentiation and the visual amplification differentiating logics. Aesthetically, it is the elegance[4] of ordered complexity and the sense of seamless fluidity, akin to natural systems that constitute the hallmark of parametricism.

Styles as Design Research Programmes

Avant-garde styles can be interpreted and evaluated analogously to new scientific paradigms, affording a new conceptual framework and formulating new aims, methods and values. Thus a new direction for concerted research work is established.[5] Thus styles are design research programmes.[6]

Innovation in architecture proceeds via the progression of styles so understood: as the alternation between periods of cumulative advancement within a style and of periods of revolutionary transition between styles. Styles therefore represent cycles of innovation, gathering design research efforts into a collective endeavour. Here, stable self-identity is as much a necessary precondition of evolution as it is in the case of organic life. To hold on to the new principles in the face of difficulties is crucial for the chance of eventual success, something that is incompatible with an understanding of styles as transient fashions. Basic principles and methodologies need to be preserved and defended with tenacity in the face of initial difficulties and setbacks: each style has its hard core of principles and a characteristic way of tackling design problems/tasks.

The programme/style consists of methodological rules: some tell us what paths of research to avoid (negative heuristics), and others what paths to pursue (positive heuristics). Negative heuristics formulates strictures that prevent relapse into old patterns that are not fully consistent with the core; positive heuristics offers guiding principles and preferred techniques that allow the work to fast-forward in a particular direction.

Defining Heuristics and Pertinent Agendas

The defining heuristics of parametricism is fully reflected in the taboos and dogmas of contemporary avant-garde design culture:

- Negative heuristics (taboos): avoid rigid geometric primitives such as squares, triangles and circles; avoid simple repetition of elements, avoid juxtaposition of unrelated elements or systems.
- Positive heuristics (dogmas): consider all forms to be parametrically malleable; differentiate gradually (at varying rates), inflect and correlate systematically.

The current stage of development within parametricism is as much to do with the continuous advancement of the attendant computational design processes as it is due to the designer's grasp of the unique formal and organisational opportunities afforded by these processes. Parametricism can only exist via the continuous advancement and sophisticated appropriation of computational geometry. Finally, computationally advanced design techniques such as scripting (in Mel-script or Rhino-script) and parametric modelling (with tools such as GC or DP) are becoming a pervasive reality such that it is no longer possible to compete within the contemporary avant-garde architecture scene without mastering and refining them. However, the advancement of techniques should go hand in hand with the formulation of yet more ambitions and goals. The following five agendas seek to inject new aspects into the parametric paradigm and to further extend the new style's reach:

1 Parametric interarticulation of subsystems
The goal is to move from single system differentiation (for example, a swarm of facade components) to the scripted association of multiple subsystems – envelope, structure, internal subdivision, navigation void. The differentiation in any one system is correlated with differentiations in the other systems.[7]

2 Parametric accentuation
Here the goal is to enhance the overall sense of organic integration by means of correlations that favour deviation amplification rather than compensatory adaptation. The associated system should accentuate the initial differentiation such that a far richer articulation is achieved and more orienting visual information made available.

3 Parametric figuration[8]
Complex configurations in which multiple readings are latent can be constructed as a parametric model with extremely figuration-sensitive variables. Parametric variations trigger 'gestalt-catastrophes', that is, the quantitative modification of these parameters triggers qualitative shifts in the perceived configuration. Beyond object parameters, ambient parameters and observer parameters have to be integrated into the parametric system.

4 Parametric responsiveness[9]
Urban and architectural environments possess an inbuilt kinetic capacity that allows those environments to reconfigure and adapt in response to prevalent occupation patterns. The real-time registration of use patterns drives the real-time kinetic adaptation. The built environment thus acquires responsive agency at different timescales.

5 Parametric urbanism[10] – deep relationality
The assumption is that the urban massing describes a swarm formation of many buildings whereby the urban variables of mass, spacing and directionality are choreographed by scripted functions. In addition, the systematic modulation of architectural morphologies produces powerful urban effects and facilitates field orientation. The goal is deep relationality, the total integration of the evolving built environment, from urban distribution to architectural morphology, detailed tectonic articulation and interior organisation. Thus parametric urbanism might apply parametric accentuation, parametric figuration and parametric responsiveness as tools to achieve deep relationality.

Parametricist vs Modernist Urbanism
Le Corbusier's first theoretical statement on urbanism begins with a eulogy to the straight line and the right angle as means whereby man conquers nature. Famously, the first two paragraphs of *The City of Tomorrow* contrast man's way with that of the pack donkey:

Man walks in a straight line because he has a goal and knows where he is going; he has made up his mind to reach some particular place and he goes straight to it. The pack-donkey meanders along, meditates a little in his scatter-brained and distracted fashion, he zig-zags in order to avoid larger stones, or to ease the climb, or to gain a little shade; he takes the line of least resistance.[11]

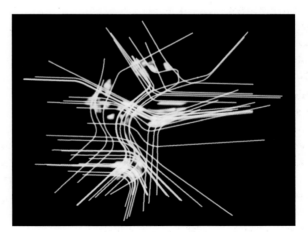

Zaha Hadid Architects, One-North Masterplan, Singapore, 2003
opposite and above: Fabric and network. This masterplan for a new mixed-used urban business district in Singapore was the first of a series of radical masterplans that led to the concept of parametric urbanism and then to the general concept of parametricism.

Le Corbusier admires the urban order of the Romans and rejects our sentimental modern-day attachment to the picturesque irregularity of the medieval city: 'The curve is ruinous, difficult and dangerous; it is a paralyzing thing;'[12] instead, he insists that 'the house, the street, the town … should be ordered; … if they are not ordered, they oppose themselves to us.'[13] Le Corbusier's limitation is not his insistence upon order but rather his limited conception of order in terms of classical geometry. Complexity theory in general, and the research of Frei Otto in particular,[14] have since taught us to recognise, measure and simulate the complex patterns that emerge from processes of self-organisation. Phenomena such as the 'pack-donkey's path' and urban patterns resulting from unplanned settlement processes can now be analysed and appreciated in terms of their underlying logic and rationality, that is, in terms of their hidden regularity and associated performative power.

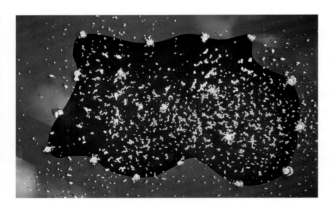

Frei Otto, Occupation with simultaneous distancing and attracting forces, Institute for Lightweight Structures (ILEK), Stuttgart, Germany, 1992
Analogue models for the material computation of structural building forms (form-finding) are the hallmark of Frei Otto's research institute. The same methodology has been applied to his urban simulation work. The model shown integrates both distancing and attractive occupations by using polystyrene chips that cluster around the floating magnetic needles that maintain distance among themselves.

Le Corbusier realised that although 'nature presents itself to us as a chaos … the spirit which animates Nature is a spirit of order'.[15] However, while his understanding of nature's order was limited by the science of his day, we now have the tools to reveal the complex order of those apparently chaotic patterns by simulating their 'material computation'. In this process, parametricist sensibility gives more credit to the 'pack-donkey's path' as a form of recursive material computation than to the simplicity of clear geometries imposed in a single, sweeping gesture.

Frei Otto's pioneering research on natural structures included work on settlement patterns. He started by focusing on the distinction/relation between occupying and connecting as the two fundamental activities involved in all processes of urbanisation,[16] his analysis of existing patterns paralleled by analogue experiments modelling crucial features of the settlement process. In a pioneering experiment, to simulate distancing occupation he used magnets floating in water, while to model attractive occupation he used floating polystyrene chips. A more complex model integrates both distancing and attractive occupations such that the polystyrene chips cluster around the floating magnetic needles that maintain distance among themselves.[17] The result closely resembles the typical settlement patterns found in our real urban landscapes.[18]

With respect to processes of connection, Frei Otto distinguishes empirically three scalar levels of path networks, each with its own typical configuration: settlement path networks, territory path networks and long-distance path networks. All start as forking systems that eventually close into continuous networks. In tandem, Otto distinguishes three fundamental types of configuration: direct path networks, minimal path networks and minimising detour networks. Again, he conceives material analogues that are able to self-organise into relatively optimised solutions. To simulate minimal path networks Otto devised the soap bubble skin apparatus in which a glass plate is held over water and the minimal path system forms itself from needles.[19] To capture the optimised detour networks the famous wool-thread models[20] are able to compute a network solution between given points that optimises the relationship of total network length and the average detour factor imposed. For each set of points, and for each adopted sur-length over the theoretical direct path, an optimising solution is produced. Although no unique optimal solution exists, and each computation is different, characteristic patterns emerge in different regions of the parametric space.

Frei Otto's form-finding models bring a large number of components into a simultaneous organising force-field so that any variation of the parametric profile of any of the elements elicits a natural response from all the other elements within the system. Such quantitative adaptations often cross thresholds into emergent qualities.

Where such an associative sensitivity holds sway within a system we can talk about 'relational fields'. Relational fields comprise mutually correlated sublayers, for instance the correlation of patterns of occupation with patterns of connection. The growth process of unplanned settlement patterns does indeed oscillate continuously between moments when points of occupation generate paths and paths

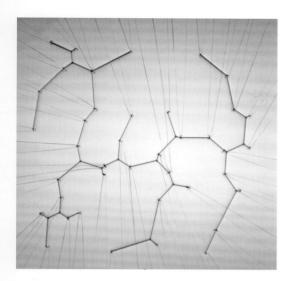

Frei Otto, Apparatus for computing minimal path systems, Institute for Lightweight Structures (ILEK), Stuttgart, 1988
The analogue model finds the minimal path system, that is, the system connects a distributed set of given points, thus the overall length of the path system is minimised. Each point is reached but there is a considerable imposition of detours between some pairs of points. The system is a tree (branching system) without any redundant connections.

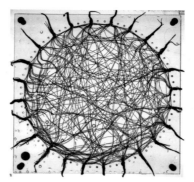 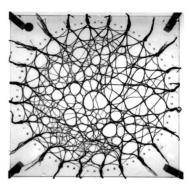

Marek Kolodziejczyk, Wool-thread model to compute optimised detour path networks, Institute for Lightweight Structures (ILEK), Stuttgart, 1991
Depending on the adjustable parameter of the thread's sur-length, the apparatus – through the fusion of threads – computes a solution that significantly reduces the overall length of the path system while maintaining a low average detour factor.

> Parametricist urbanism aims to construct new field logics that operate via the mutually accentuating correlation of multiple urban systems: fabric modulation, street systems, a system of open spaces.

in turn attract occupation. The continuous differentiation of the path network – linear stretches, forks, crossing points – correlates with the continuous differentiation of the occupying fabric in terms of its density, programmatic type and morphology. The organising/ articulating capacity of such relational fields is striking, particularly in comparison with the grid of the modern American city, which is undifferentiated and therefore non-adaptive. Its 'freedom' is now limiting: it leads to arbitrary juxtapositions that result in visual chaos.

Modernism was founded on the concept of universal space. Parametricism differentiates fields. Space is empty. Fields are full, as if filled with a fluid medium. We might think of liquids in motion, structured by radiating waves, laminal flows and spiralling eddies. Swarms have also served as paradigmatic analogues for the field-concept: swarms of buildings that drift across the landscape. There are no platonic, discrete figures or zones with sharp outlines. Within fields only regional field qualities matter: biases, drifts, gradients, and perhaps conspicuous singularities such as radiating centres. Deformation no longer spells the breakdown of order, but the inscription of information. Orientation in a complex, differentiated field affords navigation along vectors of transformation. The contemporary condition of arriving in a metropolis for the first time, without prior hotel arrangements and without a map, might instigate this kind of field-navigation. Imagine there are no more landmarks to hold on to, no axes to follow, no more boundaries to cross.

Parametricist urbanism aims to construct new field logics that operate via the mutually accentuating correlation of multiple urban systems: fabric modulation, street systems, a system of open spaces. The agenda of deep relationality implies that the fabric modulation also extends to the tectonic articulation. Both massing and fenestration, if each in its own way, might be driven by sunlight orientation, producing a mutual enhancement of the visual orienting effect. Thus local perceptions (of the facade) can provide clues to the relative position within the global system of the urban massing. The location and articulation of building entrances might be correlated with the differentiated urban navigation system,[21] a correlation that might even extend to the internal circulation. This concept of deep relationality might also operate in reverse so that, for example, the internal organisation of a major institutional building might lead to multiple entrances that in turn trigger adaptations within the urban navigation system. It is important that such laws of correlation are adhered to across sufficiently large urban stretches.

Implementing Parametricist Urbanism

The urban implementation of parametricism is still in its infancy. However, Zaha Hadid Architects was able to win a series of international masterplanning competitions with schemes that embody the style's key features. The projects include the 200-hectare (494-acre) One-North Masterplan for a mixed-use business park in Singapore; Soho City in Beijing, comprising 2.5 million square metres (26.9 million square feet) of residential and retail programme; the mixed-use masterplan for Bilbao including the river's island and both opposing embankments; and the Kartal-Pendik Masterplan,[22] a mixed-use urban field of 55 hectares (136 acres) with 6 million square metres (64.6 million square feet) of gross buildable area comprising all programmatic components of a city.

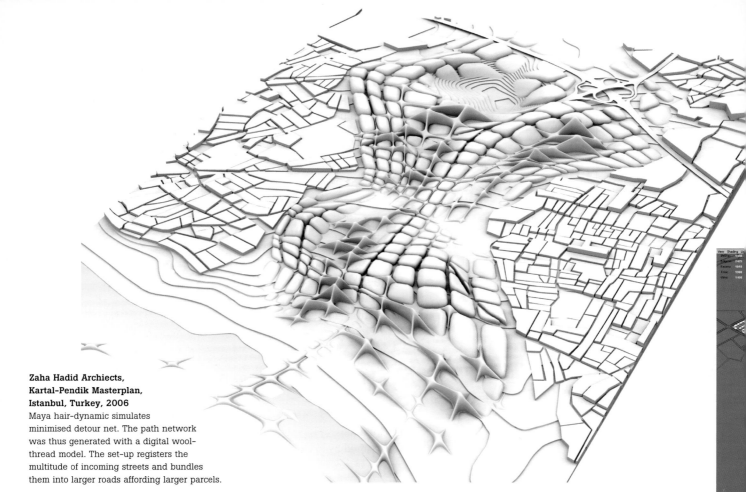

**Zaha Hadid Archiects,
Kartal–Pendik Masterplan,
Istanbul, Turkey, 2006**
Maya hair–dynamic simulates
minimised detour net. The path network
was thus generated with a digital wool–
thread model. The set–up registers the
multitude of incoming streets and bundles
them into larger roads affording larger parcels.

The Kartal-Pendik project requires the design of a subcentre on Istanbul's Asian side to reduce pressure on the city's historic core. The site is being reclaimed from industrial estates and is flanked by the small-grain fabric of suburban towns. Respecting the parametricist taboo on unmediated juxtapositions, the adjacent context, in particular the incoming lines of circulation, was taken as an important input for the generation of the urban geometry. Maya's hair dynamic tool achieved a parametrically tuned bundling of the incoming paths into larger roads enclosing larger sites such that the resultant lateral path system exhibits the basic properties of Frei Otto's minimising detour network. The longitudinal direction was imposed via a primary artery with a series of subsidiary roads running parallel. The result is a hybrid of minimising detour network and deformed grid. At the same time, Zaha Hadid Architects worked with two primary fabric typologies, towers and perimeter blocks, each conceived as a generative component or geno-type that allows for a wide range of pheno-typical variation. The towers, conceived as cross towers, were placed on the crossing points to accentuate the path network. The perimeter block inversely correlates height with parcel area so that courtyards morph into internal atria as sites get smaller and blocks get taller. Blocks split along the lines of the secondary path network, which together with the accentuating height differentiation, allows the block type to be assimilated to the cross-tower type. 'Pseudo-towers' are formed at some crossing points by pulling up the four corners of the four blocks that meet at such a corner.

opposite top: Global Maya model. The model features the interarticulation between cross towers and perimeter blocks as well as the affiliation to the surrounding fabric. The correlation of global width to global height can also be observed.

below: Scripting calligraphy block patterns. Various scripts were developed that configure the perimeter blocks depending on parcel size, proportion and orientation. The script also allowed for random variations regarding the introduction of openings within blocks.

bottom: New cityscape. The Kartal-Penkik plan incorporates a vast quarry that becomes the largest item in a system of parks that are spread throughout the urban field. The rhythmic flow of the urban fabric gives a sense of organic cohesion.

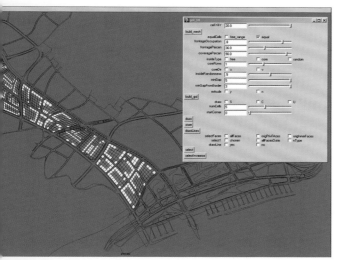

Thus, an overall sense of continuity is achieved despite the entire process having started from two quite distinct urban typologies. In terms of global height regulation, and aside from local dependency of height on parcel size, the project correlates the conspicuous build-up of height with the lateral width of the overall site. Parametricist applications thus allow the rhythm of urban peaks to index the rhythm of the widening and narrowing of the urban field. The result is an elegant, coherently differentiated cityscape that facilitates navigation through its lawful (rule-based) constitution and through the architectural accentuation of both global and local field properties.

It may well be possible to implement this design for the Kartal-Pendik project assuming the imposition of strict planning guidelines using building lines and height regulation. Political and private buy-ins are also required. Moreover, all constituencies need to be convinced that the individual restrictions placed upon all sites really deliver collective value: the unique character and coherent order of the urban field from which all players benefit if compliance guidelines can be enforced. Ordered complexity here replaces the monotony of older planned developments and the disorienting visual chaos that marks virtually all unregulated contemporary city expansions.

To go further. In terms of the concept of deep relationality, Zaha Hadid Architects must extend its involvement from urbanism to architecture; only then can the desired accentuating correlations be intensified by involving the systematic modulation of tectonic features. For instance, in terms of the 'calligraphy blocks' (a third perimeter block variation that has been designed both to open up the interior of

parcels and to cross parcels), a continuous facade differentiation that leads from the street side to the courtyard on the basis of an initial distinction between external and internal facades is used. Other moments of deep articulation are the coordination of landscape and public spaces, and the correlation of the secondary path system with the disposition of internal navigation systems.

Doubts may be experienced when confronted with the possibility of designing an urban field of up to 6 million square metres (64.6 million square feet) gross area with a single design team. Are we overstretching our capacity here? The answer is, no. The more often we are confronted with the task of designing large-scale developments of this kind, the more confident we become that the tools and strategies we are deploying under the banner of parametricism can indeed deliver something that produces a decisive surplus value when compared with the usual alternative of uncoordinated, arbitrary juxtapositions. The contemporary choice of typologies, construction options and styles is simply too wide to expect the underlying pragmatic logics to become legible. The result is a cacophony of pure difference. Parametricism is able to further coordinate pragmatic concerns and articulate them with all their rich differentiations and relevant associations while the danger of overriding real-life richness is minimised because variety and adaptiveness are written into the very genetic make-up of this new style. ◄

opposite: Calligraphy blocks – tectonic detail. The articulation of the facades is a function of the location within the urban field. The exterior of the blocks is given a heavier relief than the interior. Where a block opens up and the public space flows into the private courtyard, a semi-private zone is articulated via the gradient transformation between the outer and inner articulation.
below: Close-up of cross towers. The cross towers produce the urban peaks. Through their ground-level articulation these tower complexes participate in the creation of a continuous urban fabric that frames the streets and occasionally widens the street space into semi-public plazas. This is achieved while maintaining total continuity between the podium-like ground fabric and the shafts of the towers.

Notes

1. ZHA and AADRL together form just one node within this fast-growing network.

2. Also, we should not forget that the desire for an architecture marked by a complex, fluid, nature-like continuity was clearly expressed before the new digital tools had entered the arena: see Zaha Hadid's work of the late 1980s and Eisenman/Lynn's folding projects of the early 1990s. (This point also indicates that we are confronted with a new style and not merely new techniques.) Since then we have witnessed a conceptual radicalisation and increased formal sophistication along the lines previously set out, leading to the emergence of a powerful new style.

3. The credit for coining this key slogan goes to Greg Lynn and Jeff Kipnis.

4. For a pertinent concept of elegance that is related to the visual resolution of complexity, see Patrik Schumacher, 'Arguing for Elegance', in Ali Rahim and Hina Jamelle, *AD Elegance*, Vol 77, No 1, Jan/Feb 2007.

5. This interpretation of styles is valid only with respect to the avant-garde phase of any style.

6. It is important to distinguish research programmes in the literal sense of institutional research plans from the meta-scientific conception of research programmes that has been introduced into the philosophy of science: whole new research traditions that are directed by a new fundamental theoretical framework. It is this latter concept that is utilised here to reinterpret the concept of style. See Imre Lakatos, *The Methodology of Scientific Research Programmes*, Cambridge University Press (Cambridge), 1978.

7. Parametricism involves a conceptual shift from part-to-whole relationships to component-system relationships, system-to-system relationships and system-subsystem relationships. Parametricism prefers open systems that always remain incomplete; that is, without establishing wholes. As the density of associations increases, so components may become associated in multiple systems. The correlation of initially independent systems implies the formation of a new encompassing system.

8. 'Parametric figuration' featured in teachings at the Yale School of Architecture, the University of Applied Arts in Vienna and in the author's studio at the AADRL.

9. 'Parametric responsiveness' was at the heart of our three-year design research agenda 'Responsive Environments' at the AADRL in London from 2001 to 2004.

10. 'Parametric Urbanism' is the title of our recently completed design research cycle at the AADRL, from 2005 to 2008.

11. Le Corbusier, *The City of Tomorrow and its Planning*, Dover Publications (New York), 1987, p 5. Translated from the French original: *Urbanisme*, Paris, 1925.

12. Ibid, p 8.

13. Ibid, p 15.

14. Frei Otto might be considered as the sole true precursor of parametricism.

15. Le Corbusier, op cit, p 18.

16. Frei Otto, *Occupying and Connecting – Thoughts on Territories and Spheres of Influence with Particular Reference to Human Settlement*, Edition Axel Menges (Stuttgart/London), 2009.

17. Ibid, p 45.

18. Within the AADRL research agenda of 'Parametric Urbanism' we too always started with material analogues that were then transposed into the domain of digitally simulated self-organisation.

19. Frei Otto, op cit, p 64.

20. Marek Kolodziejczyk, 'Thread Model, Natural–Spontaneous Formation of Branches', in SFB 230, *Natural Structures – Principles, Strategies, and Models in Architecture and Nature*, Proceedings of the 2nd International Symposium of the Sonderforschungsbereich 230, Stuttgart, 1991, p 139.

21. This is what Zaha Hadid Architects imposed within the urban guidelines for the Singapore masterplan.

22. Zaha Hadid Architects, design team: Zaha Hadid, Patrik Schumacher, Saffet Bekiroglu, Daewa Kang, Daniel Widrig, Bozana Komljenovic, Sevil Yazici, Vigneswaran Ramaraju, Brian Dale, Jordan Darnell, Elif Erdine, Melike Altinisik, Ceyhun Baskin, Inanc Eray, Fluvio Wirz, Gonzalo Carbajo, Susanne Lettau, Amit Gupta, Marie-Perrine Placais, Jimena Araiza.

Experiments in Associative Urbanism

'THERE HAS NEVER BEEN A MORE CRUCIAL TIME TO CHALLENGE, REASSESS AND PROPOSE ALTERNATIVES TO CONVENTIONAL URBAN MASTERPLANNING AND ITS ASSOCIATED CONVENTIONS, TYPES AND STANDARDS.' TOM VEREBES DESCRIBES HOW THE DESIGN RESEARCH LABORATORY (DRL) AT THE ARCHITECTURAL ASSOCIATION IN LONDON HAS EMPLOYED A PARAMETRIC APPROACH TO URBANISM THAT INVESTIGATES HOW ASSOCIATIVE DESIGN SYSTEMS CAN CONTROL LOCAL DYNAMIC INFORMATION FLOWS THROUGH INTERACTIVE SYSTEMS, SPACES AND INTERFACES.

Ancient cities were developed, updated and retrofitted primarily in relation to military and civic infrastructural requirements for their sustenance. Whether exemplified by Hausmann's boulevards of Paris, or the 20th-century expansion and widening of the ring roads of Beijing, urban infrastructure has been designed to impress – and even to control – its citizens and would-be invaders by its efficient infrastructural and military network. During the Cold War, the freeways of American cities were planned to not only link new suburbs to the pre-existing city centres, but also to provide a national network for a get-away plan should their centres be the target of a nuclear strike. Contemporary urbanism continues to be organised by networks of interrelated systems, and this relational paradigm assumes the city to be a living expression of the parametric systems deployed in our modern world.

Masterplanning strategies that seek an enduring final state of urban completion tend to lead to dysfunctional cities with limited capability to adapt and change. The DRL's design research work on relational forms of urbanism has sought alternatives to conventional urban masterplanning based on stable typologies and teleological final states, instead working towards designing an evolving city with capacities of adaptation to future contingencies. Given the current instability of global urbanisation, there has never been a more crucial time to challenge, reassess and propose alternatives to conventional urban masterplanning and its associated conventions, types and standards. Cities today may still be made from mineral and geological matter, but they are shaped by the embedding of invisible informational control systems, whereby the augmented cybernetic apparatus manages the quotidian fluxes, flows and pulses of the city. In this sense, the city is alive, rather than dead and inert, which is also evident in the ways in which cities evolve and adapt to dynamic contextual conditions.

The vehicles inherent to our understanding of contemporary urbanism are design techniques capable of managing the immensely complex qualities of interaction, communication and exchange that characterise 21st-century urbanism. Our parametric approach to urbanism addresses the ways in which associative design systems can control local dynamic information to effect and adjust larger urban life-processes by embedding intelligence into the formation, organisation and performance of urban spaces, uses, activities, interfaces, structures and infrastructures.

Not limited to the scale of urbanism being always and already relational, this position implicitly seeks to formalise coherent yet heterogeneous and differentiated forms of architectural, structural and systemic organisation and expression. The repercussions of parametric design may indeed surpass the mere shaping of a new style, and today's fascination with complex, curvilinear form is increasingly propagating and consolidating earlier 20th-century experiments by Mendelsohn, Kiessler, Saarinen, Gaudí and others. Differing from the soft, plastic, materially driven experiments of these deviants of Modernism, whose place in the official histories of architecture is awkward, at best, and more often excluded and branded as Expressionism, our current obsession with algorithmic design marks a profound paradigm shift. The creative enterprise now rests less with the individual gesture, and instead in the refinement of code-based design methods whose design outcomes oscillate from the accidental to the intentional. These new algorithmic methods clearly intensify the interaction of the designer with a digital model-space, yielding not only one singular designed object but, rather, where each design scheme is now just one instance of a multiplicity of possible outcomes.

DRL Craft_Id team (Tutors: Patrik Schumacher and Christos Passas; Students: Victoria Goldstein, Xingzhu Hu, Ludovico Lombardi and Du Yu), Parametric Urbanism 2, DRL v.10 2006–2008
Aerial view of the masterplan, indicating the post-Shanghai Expo proposal for the site, developed with three primary architectural typologies – fields of differentiated towers; low density yet permanent Expo and cultural facilities; and landscape spaces, also reserved for further development.

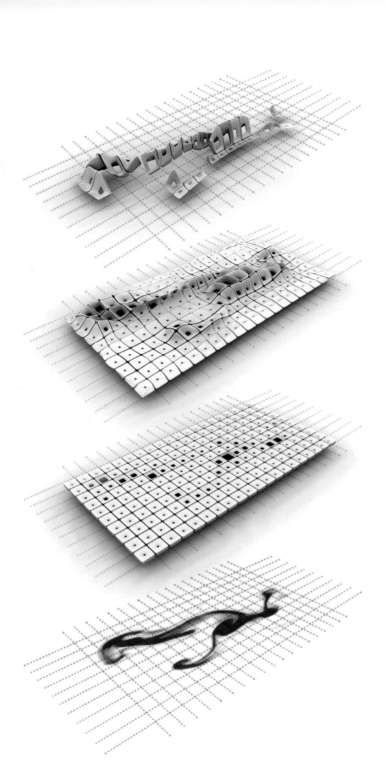

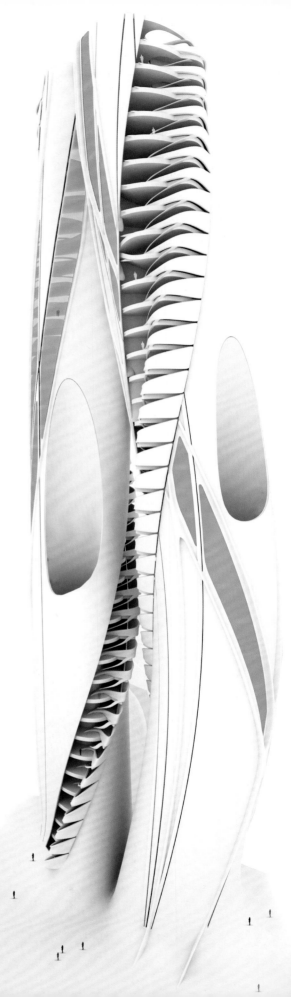

DRL Craft_Id team (Tutors: Patrik Schumacher and Christos Passas; Students: Victoria Goldstein, Xingzhu Hu, Ludovico Lombardi and Du Yu), Parametric Urbanism 2, DRL v.10 2006–2008

above: Series of diagrams describing the design development of initial fluid simulations in Maya, followed by successive stages of design development and post-production scripting and modelling, increasingly resolving and refining the model as a design proposal informed by other spatial, structural and circulatory parameters.
right: Design development of a prototypical high-rise tower, demonstrating the relational spatial systems deployed as a non-extruded model, including solid envelopes, curved curtain walls revealing floor strata, and atrium voids.

Although the current generation of architects continues to be euphoric about complex architectural spaces, as well as the potential to manage the integration of engineering, fabrication and site operations via building information modelling (BIM) and construction delivery systems which facilitate the updating of ongoing dynamic information during design and construction stages, the ramifications of these new design and production tools for urbanism have remained untheorised and nor have they been exercised in practice. The potential to update, revise and alter a masterplan in real time, over durations of months and years, sees to revolutionise the discipline and profession of urban planning. In addition, non-standard file-to-factory methods can be conceived beyond the polite scale of bespoke, one-off buildings, to question, and even depose, the hegemony of repetitive production on the scale of the city. Proposed here is the mass-customisation of urbanism, where coherent formations acquiesce uniformity for the numerical control of information-based, differentiated urban order. The DRL's design teams have been developing such proposals for a variety of scales, demonstrating the relational logic of urbanism, architecture and smaller-scale building systems.

Concluding nine years of urban research on various sites in London, the first cycle of the Parametric Urbanism project (DRL v.9 2005–2007) deployed a palette of advanced parametric tools in the development of multiscalar proposals for the Lea Valley and Thames Gateway in and around the London 2012 Olympic site. Located in the birthplace of the Industrial Revolution, where pre-Victorian technology transformed the Lea Valley, the site is now post-industrial brownfield wasteland, quickly being transformed by the regenerative force of the Olympic and ancillary developments. The DRL Flotsam team's proposal for the International Broadcasting Centre/Media Press Centre (IBC/MPC) for the London

DRL Flotsam team (Tutor: Yusuke Obuchi; Students: Öznur Erboga, Lillie Liu, Theodora Ntatsopoulou and Victor Orive), Parametric Urbanism 1, DRL v.9 2005–2007
Urban site diagram demonstrating how the three-dimensional network of the oscillating architectural surface organisation is integrated into the context of Stratford and the Olympic Park. Key contextual connections and destinations are indicated.

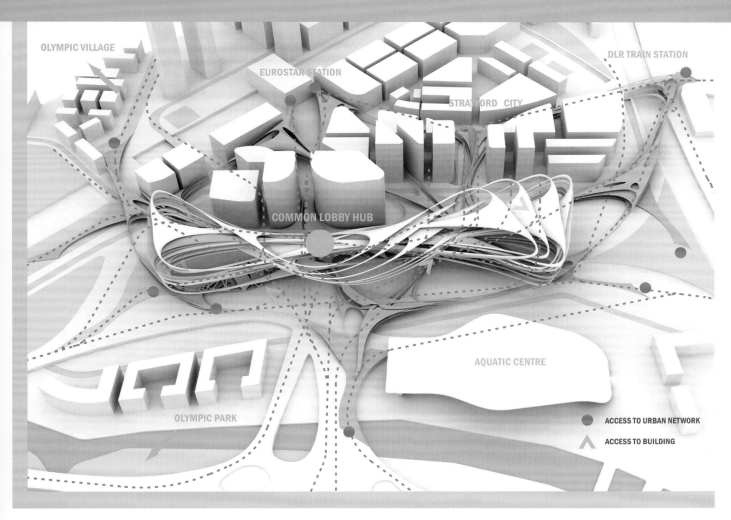

DRL Flotsam team (Tutor: Yusuke Obuchi; Students: Öznur Erboga, Lillie Liu, Theodora Ntatsopoulou and Victor Orive), Parametric Urbanism 1, DRL v.9 2005–2007

below: Series of scripted attractor diagrams in Maya, and their associated abstract, prototypical spaces, which served as the generative basis of the later design development of the proposal.

opposite: View of the pedestrian approach to the International Broadcasting Centre/Media Press Centre building, from Stratford station, indicating the integration of circulation, facade panellisation and building structure.

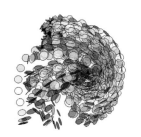

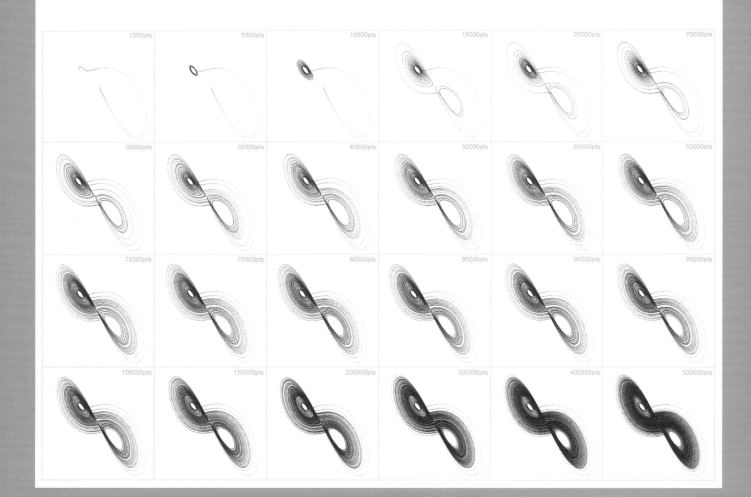

2012 Olympics distributes more than 100,000 square metres (1,076,391 square feet) of cellular spaces in a network organisation channelling movement between Stratford and the Olympic Park. As an alternative to the large black box, the project's porous plan embeds the building in an urban landscape. Its machinic design methodology deploys point-clouds generated algorithmically in simulations of strange attractors, giving rise to both a vertical and a horizontal interweaving of private and shared spaces. Given that these iterative design techniques can perform the same operation at different scales, the project can simultaneously address architectural and urban issues.

As a seemingly natural extension of the international make-up of the staff and student population of the programme, DRL v.10 2006–2008 then shifted towards the design of innovative forms of accelerated urbanisation for the Expo 2010 site in Shanghai, one of the fastest expanding and densifying cities in the world. The Expo proposals were briefed with direct consultation by the masterplanning team of Expo 2010, in a workshop with Studio 6 from the Urban Design and Planning Institute, Tongji University College of Architecture and Urban Planning. Far from a celebration of impermanence and ephemerality, the Craft_Id team dealt with questions of environmental, economic, cultural and social endurance within the particular context of China's showcase of rapid urbanisation. Using computational fluid dynamics as a tool for achieving highly integrated, coherent systems, the project explored alternatives to the urban grid in the site for the Shanghai Expo. Density, verticality and vast open spaces are correlated as parametrically generated patterns of self-similar figures for a variety of programmes, landscapes, infrastructures and Expo pavilions. Behavioural patterns and information embedded in fluid dynamics are integrated into the composition of spaces and forms. Based on gestalt principles of multiple latent readings, these perceptual patterns install variety within the elements of the proposed cityscape while maintaining an overall sense of order.

These kinds of coherent, rule-based forms of distribution were initially observed in the flow of viscous fluids spreading across a surface, and the urbanism that emerges from these observations aims to optimise the configuration of the entire site alongside specific local conditions.

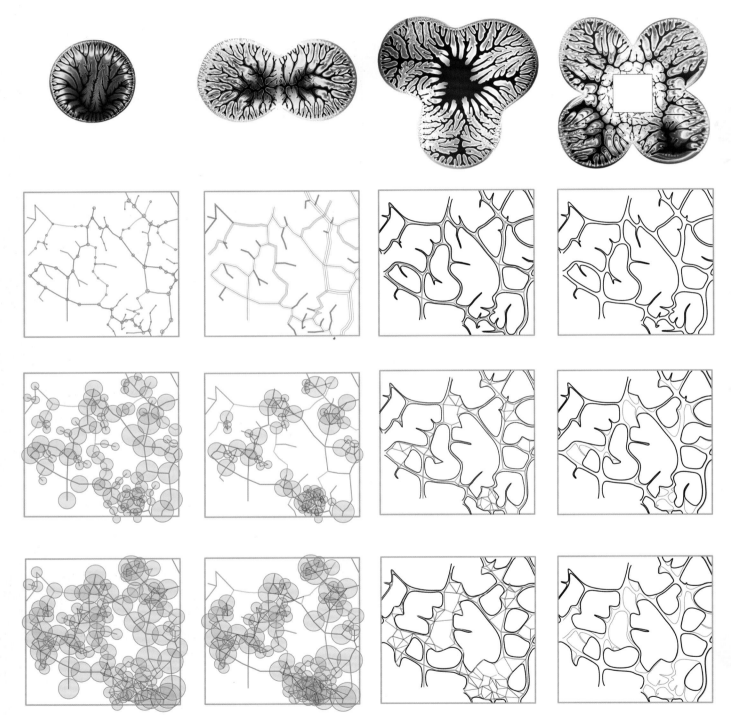

DRL Egloo team (Tutor: Theodore Spyropoulos; Students: Pankaj Chaudhary, Jawalant Mahadevwala, Mateo Riestra and Drago Vodanovic), Parametric Urbanism 2, DRL v.10 2006–2008
Top: Material experiments of glue behaviours in Petri dishes, relating single, double, triple and quadruple nodes, and their associated branching organisations, distributing glue and air. *Bottom*: Series of diagrams assessing the neighbourhood qualities of integration and segregation of spaces, using space syntax software, in relation to hierarchies of varied routing widths.

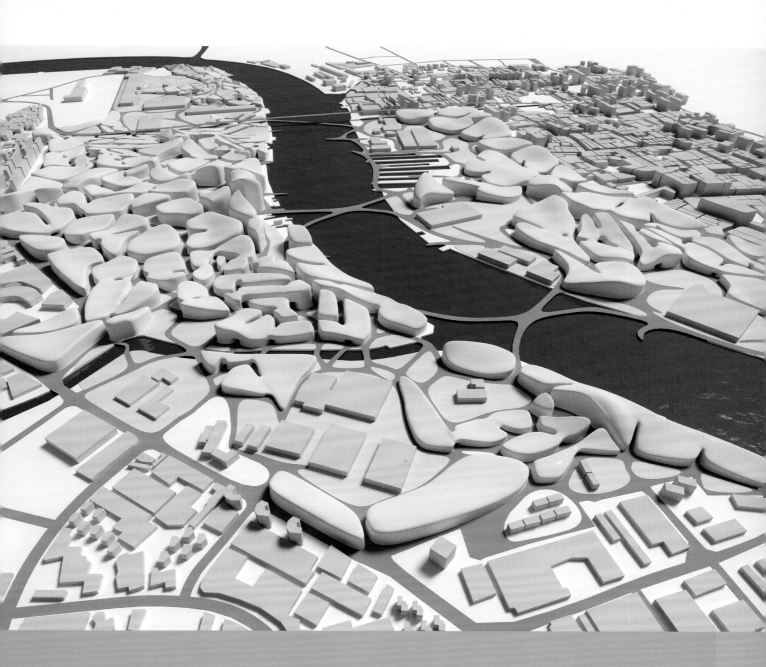

In another project for a large-scale mixed-use housing zone for Shanghai, also for the Expo 2010 site, the DRL Egloo team developed a proposal with an algorithm simulating growth in natural forms. Space syntax software was then applied in the analysis of the performance of branching systems. These kinds of coherent, rule-based forms of distribution were initially observed in the flow of viscous fluids spreading across a surface, and the urbanism that emerges from these observations aims to optimise the configuration of the entire site alongside specific local conditions. Between them, self-organised systems control the relation and distribution of varied densities, programmes and orientations.

Aerial view of the final post–Expo 2010 masterplan. The coherent, sinuous massing diagram was generated from an associative model of urban circulation and interior architectural circulation, organising neighbourhoods with differential integration and segregation.

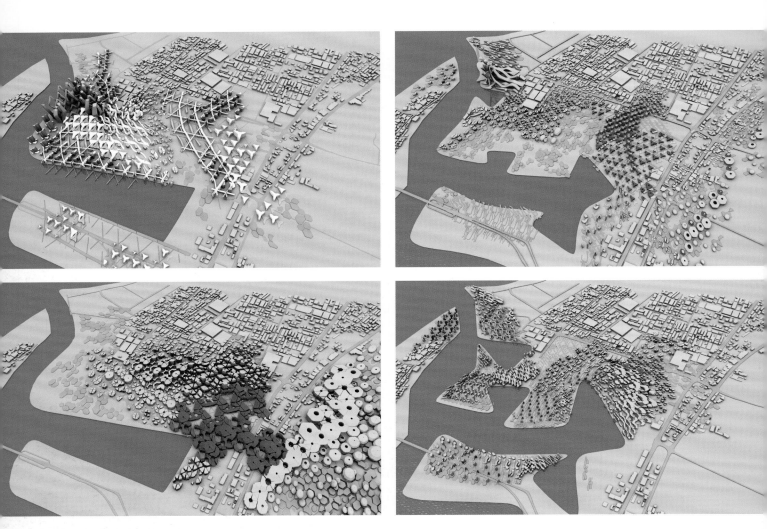

**DRL Sahra team (Tutor: Tom Verebes; Students: Saif Almasri,
Suryansh Chandra and Peter Sovinc), Parametric Urbanism 3, DRL v.11 2007–2009**
Four different scenarios of urban growth and development of Ras Al-Khaimah in the UAE – biasing
tourism, finance, local housing, and all three programmes equally – played out in a parametric
scripted model of massing, and their associated open spaces and circulatory networks, generated
from dynamic colour fields driving Grasshopper, a plug-in for Rhino. This approach to urbanism
assumes a variability and adaptability of a masterplan (and its systems) to changing future criteria.

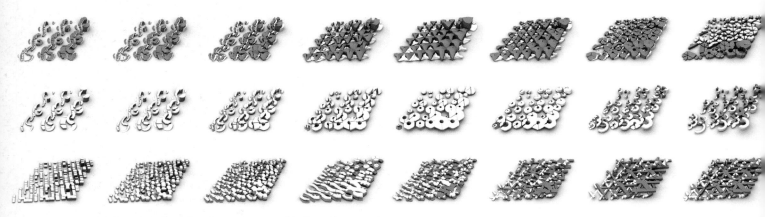

Morphing transformations of massing diagrams, generated in Maya, demonstrating
the potential to order space with coherent yet differentiated systems. This approach
argues for a vast array of architectural difference, while maintaining a legible,
negotiated density, open-interior massing ratio and varied floor area ratio (FAR).

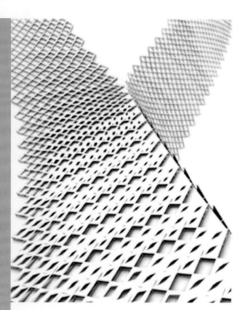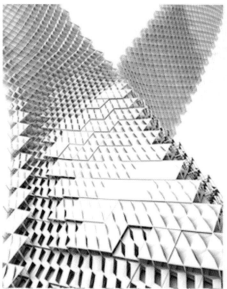

Parametric design systems which bias transformation of components, rather than their mere repetition, as applied to the design problem of generating diverse yet coherent facade patterns.

Global urbanisation is developing at unprecedented rates, scales and densities, with over half the world's population living in cities. In the third and final cycle of Parametric Urbanism, DRL v.11, which was concluded in January 2009, the DRL explored global urbanisation and the diverse contingencies of four sites located in New York, Moscow, São Paolo and Ras Al-Khaimah in the United Arab Emirates. The studios investigated diverse strategies for radical urban development and transformation, aiming to progress from familiar models of emblematic internationalism towards new iterative organisational models for high-density urbanism, specified and differentiated to local contextual forces in four cities in four continents. Ras Al-Khaimah has been competing with Dubai and Abu Dhabi in the race for rampant urbanisation, shaped and driven by the abundance of oil, vehicular urbanism and air conditioning, with little consideration for pedestrians, public transportation or the environment. As a critique of this globalised form of urbanisation, the Sahra team's project proposes a gradient of massing and movement figures, densities, proximities and interconnectivities, on a site stretching from the seafront to the inland desert. A vast catalogue of architectural morphologies, along with their respective systems – envelopes, structures, floors and atria, and cores and circulation – are generated through vector-based climatological and urban parameters (sunlight, wind, view, programming and routing), managing the penetration of natural light in a super-deep and dense built environment.

The projects featured here – just four out of a total of 33 that have focused on the Parametric Urbanism research agenda – highlight some of the salient design outcomes and discoveries that have resulted from the DRL's research. From 2005, the lab's design teams began importing associative design tools and systems to investigate their implications on problems, briefs and locales of urbanism. Rather than assuming contemporary urbanism requires parametric tools, the teams quickly understood how cities have in fact always been relational expressions of social, political, economic, geographic and topographic conditions and contexts. Parametric Urbanism is not a new concept; rather, it is a new computational form that is yet to be built. ⚙

The Architectural Association's Design Research Lab (DRL) is an open-source, post-professional MArch design laboratory dedicated to a systematic exploration of new design tools, systems and discourses. Understanding design as a vehicle of research, through the ways in which design projects are conceptualised, developed and documented, the DRL emphasises analytic, process-oriented forms of design experimentation guided by longer-term research agendas. This research-driven mode of architectural experimentation emerged concurrently in a decade which has seen the embedding of digital design and communications networks into the architect's design studio. The application of new forms of associative logic have been applied towards the conception and materialisation of comprehensive design proposals, focused on three major design research agendas over three cycles of students since 1997. Between 2005 and 2009, four parallel design studios, totalling 121 masters' students in 33 design teams, distributed in four studios, have worked collaboratively on the Parametric Urbanism agenda, led by Yusuke Obuchi, Patrik Schumacher/Christos Passas, Theodore Spyropoulos and Tom Verebes, and supported by a team of workshop and technical tutors.

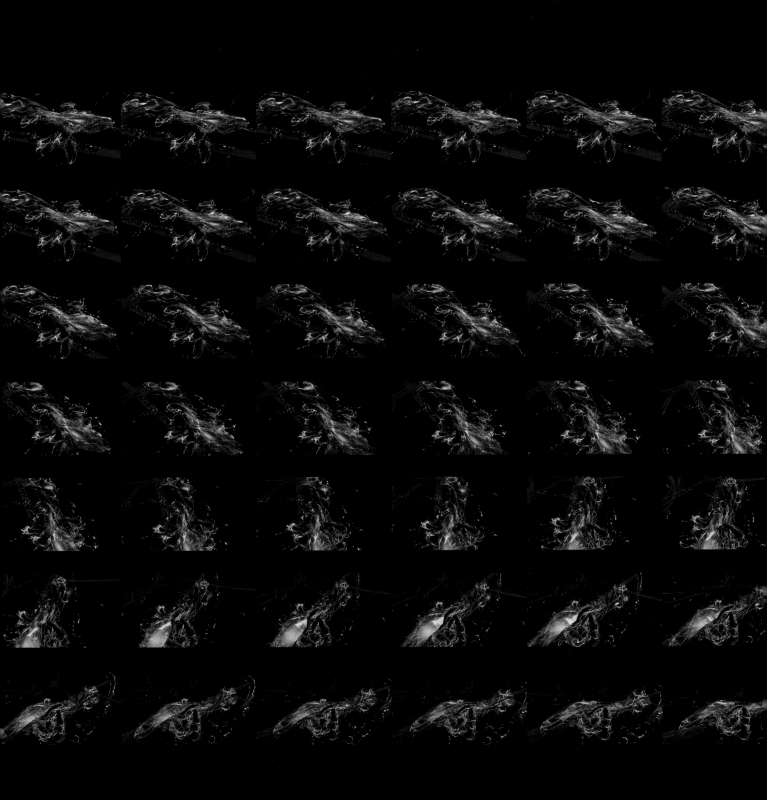

CHLOROFILIA, THE

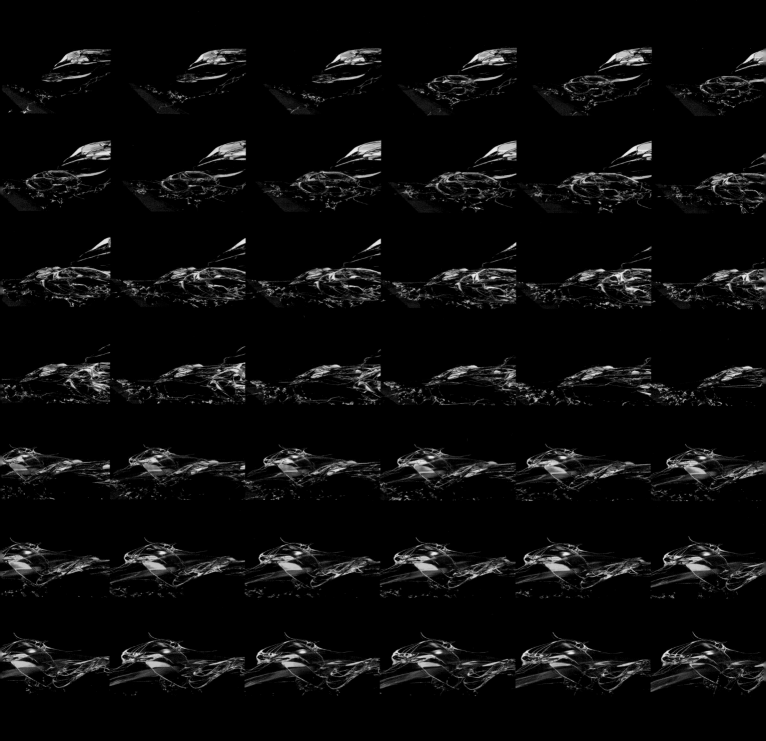

LOS ANGELES JUNGLE

In psychology, perverse behaviour is deemed pathological by its deviation from 'normal' desire. However, the definition of perversion has shifted considerably over time. Indeed, it has always been a contested category of meaning. Today, psychologists generally refer to non-traditional behaviour as a form of 'deviation' or, in cases where the specific object of arousal is unusual, as 'paraphilia'.

When, in 2007, the History Channel invited architects to explore the future of the US metropolis, **Hernan Diaz Alonso** chose the medium of film to explore the dark side of the city of angels. **Neil Leach** asked Alonso how he went about challenging the conventional masterplan and provoking with his dystopian view.

The year is 2106. Welcome to the city of Chlorofilia. In a world of global warming, where the melting icecaps have forced sea levels up dramatically, Los Angeles is put under threat. Levees hold back the rising waters, but eventually in 2023 an earthquake – the 'big one' – destroys the levees and Los Angeles is flooded, except for three areas of high land that become islands. Yet out of this apocalyptic scene a new Los Angeles emerges – Chlorofilia.

A jungle overtakes the city, and turns it into a living, breathing, self-sustaining, self-protecting environment. The jungle is a living surface, a cultural membrane. It is an environment that can grow and respond to various impulses and needs. It is never finished, and constantly adapting. It is informed by a new thought, a new wisdom, a new understanding about humankind and their place in the environment. In Chlorofilia a new species of architecture has developed: one with its own intelligence that can evolve on its own, and change as it needs to; one that brings nature back into the information loop. Forget bricks and think of cells – cells that can reform, recombine and reconnect in different ways, according to their own internal intelligence.

But beneath the cosy utopian world that the project seems to be promoting, there is another, darker side. 'This was of course a project that was challenging the notion of the masterplan,' says Hernan Diaz Alonso. 'It was about how things would happen if they were out of control. It was a provocation – a movie that was presented as a fake documentary, a future history of what might have happened. While everyone else was dreaming about the future through a kind of developer mentality, as though the future would be a theme park, we were trying to radicalise it. We were trying to push things into an insane territory.

'We were interested in the idea of perversion, and in the idea that there is no longer any distinction between perversity and beauty. Even the name "Chlorofilia" was dreamt up as an allusion to paedophilia. We were not talking about some cosy environmentally friendly world of tree hugging. This is a dystopian technological world in which the distinction between who we are and technology has evaporated.

'The project functions as a cinematic game: where there is no narrative, there are only active behaviours and emergent interactive aesthetics between the city and the perversions. Behaviours are in constant actualisation. The fundamental difference asserted in this proposal rests in the notion that the form and image of the project attempt to embody "how" one might engage information and culture itself, as opposed to exclusively repeating familiar forms of the past and representing a static permanence within the body of the city.'

Chlorofilia, then, is a form of science-fiction tongue-in-cheek provocation. Yet it is one that in a very real way points towards the professional alliances that might have a major impact on the future of architectural production. The project was a collaboration between Xefirotarch, a progressive architectural practice, and Imaginary Forces, a visionary special-effects company based in Hollywood and working largely for the movie industry. Are we witnessing here the birth of a new genre – a new collaborative synergy between architecture and the movie industry in an age that has been colonised increasingly by the cinematographic imagination? ∆

The Chlorofilia project is a collaboration between Hernan Diaz Alonso of Xefirotarch and Peter Frankfurt of Imaginary Forces
(http://www.imaginaryforces.com/archive/alphabetical/368).

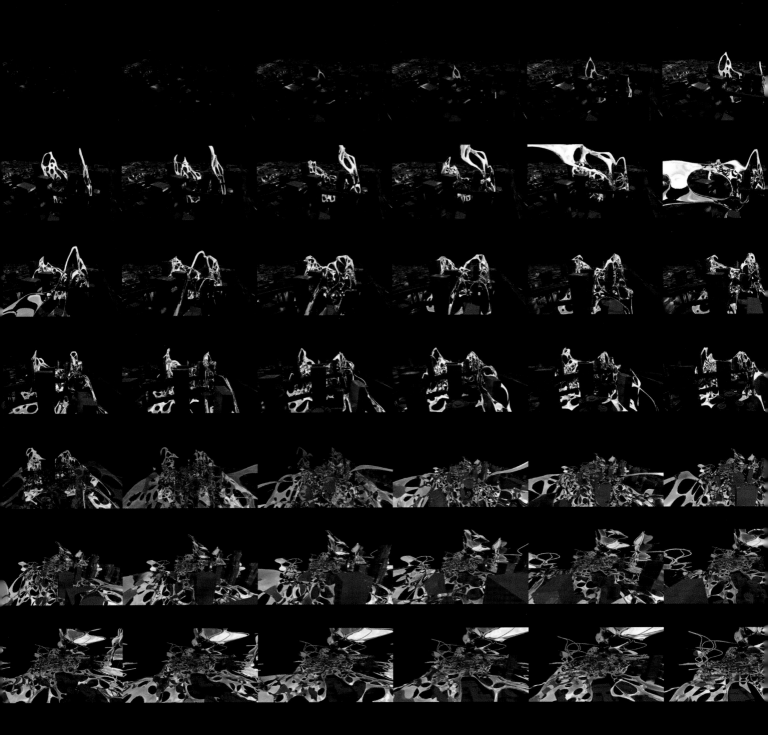

'This new species has mutated the way man perceives architecture be applied to how we exist in this world, how we build up the

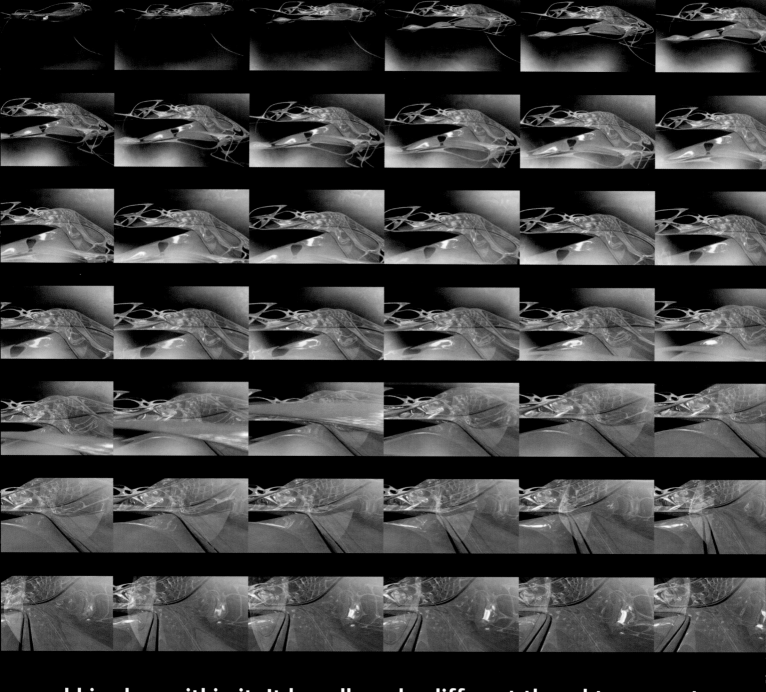

and his place within it. It has allowed a different thought process to
world around us, and how the world builds itself.'

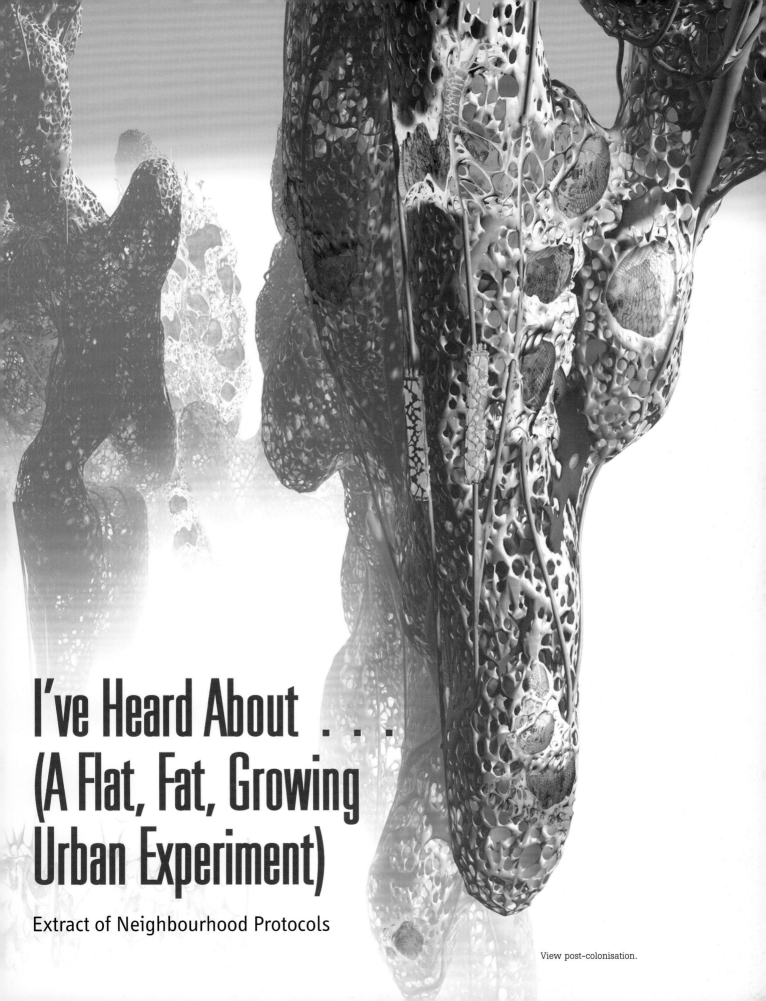

I've Heard About . . . (A Flat, Fat, Growing Urban Experiment)

Extract of Neighbourhood Protocols

View post-colonisation.

Urban models are conventionally planned and intended to control urban systems. François Roche's vision is to the contrary: it is for an unpredictable organic urbanism. A biostructure develops its own adaptive behaviour, based on growth scripts and open algorithms. It is entirely reflexive, responding to human occupation and expression rather than being managed or operated at human will.

$$\xrightleftharpoons{\quad} \begin{array}{l} V_n = V_{n+2} \\ \ = V_{n+8} \end{array}$$

V_{n+1}

$\vec{u}_{n_i}$

V_{n+4}

$V_{n+3} = V_{n+5}$

$\vec{u}_{n_j}$

V_{n+6}

$$\vec{u}_t(q) = V\big(\rho_i(q), \varepsilon_i(q) \mid c(q)\big)$$

Neighbourhood protocol
Current state approved by e-pulse 25792-45-34

The urban structure 'I've heard about' is a habitable organism. It develops by means of adaptive, transitory scenarios in which the operational mode is uncertainty. It is written based on growth scripts, open algorithms, that remain permeable not only to human expressions (expressions of individuality, relational, conflictual and transactional modes, etc), but also to the most discrete data such as the chemical emissions of those who inhabit it. This biostructure becomes the visible part of human contingencies and their negotiation in real time. Due to its modes of emergence, its fabrication cannot be delegated to a political power that would deny its exchange procedures and design its contours in advance, either through mnemonics or coercion.

Generative Schemas

1 Entropies

1.0 The habitable structure is the result of an ongoing movement. It is an adaptive landscape, a biotropism based on local growth procedures that are themselves in a constant state of evolution. This is a general principle.

1.1 The primary function of the biostructure is to serve as a dwelling place. Its secondary function is to be reactive rather than proactive.

1.1.1 As an organism, the biostructure is not only receptive to human vicissitudes, it is their nerve ending.

1.2 The construction engine called Viab is a constituent part of the structure itself. It secretes the landscape where it is located and through which it moves. It is the vector of political and territorial self-determination operating in two modes: variability and viability.

1.2.1 The Viab generates the reticular structure using a process modelled on contour crafting (see [Processes]).

1.2.2 The growth of the reticular structure takes place through local accretion occurring arhythmically, not planned in advance but taking into account viability, ie all the varieties of structural constraint (see [Processes]).

1.2.3 At any given time, the construction algorithm is the same for all the engines present in the biostructure. Each Viab proceeds according to this algorithm, but conditioned by data, requests and local disturbances that are inherently variable.

1.2.3.1 Thus the variability of the Viab arises from the script that drives it, and this script itself undergoes a ceaseless reparametering as defined in [1.4].

1.3 The resulting form is uncertain and even unpredictable. It is the political antidote to the anticipatory modes that make space a system of control.

1.3.1 Consequently, the process is undeterminist.

1.3.2 Since the space involved in construction is indeterminate, it is assumed to be unfinished. If the opposite is the case, see [5.2 / 5.2.1].

1.4 The construction algorithm responds to two kinds of data inputs, internal and external.
The external inputs comprise the pre-existing urban morphology, modes of accessibility, structural limits, available natural light, the dimension and thickness of the habitable cells, the ensemble of parameters of the local biotope, etc.

The internal inputs are of two types:
1) Chemical: physiological empathy, endocrinal secretions, bodily emissions, prepsychisms. See [Self-Alienation].
2) Electronic: individualisms, personal commitments, subjectivities (information and decision-making network). See [Biopolitics].

1.4.1 The alchemy of the various inputs achieved by the construction algorithm determines the Viab's actions. The miscibility of the data is what gives rise to the collective body.

1.5 The algorithm is open source. Its variability results from experiences, sharing and negotiations. See [4.5].

1.6 The biostructure expands without eradicating the pre-existing tissues. The process does not start from a tabula rasa, nor does it lead to patrimonialisation. The structure behaves likes a graft, or better said, a parasite. It operates in previously urbanised zones, seeps into interstices, places and environments, etc.

1.7 The biostructure is regionalised. The construction algorithm takes into account the supply of raw materials as a construction variable, and depends directly on the physical qualities of the substances used.

2 Bio-Citizens

2.0 The mere fact of being present in the biostructure confers citizenship rights.
This is a general principle.

2.0.1 Consequently, the nature of the compact is territorial.

2.0.2 Citizens may reappropriate a space, extend and transform it, and even destroy it.

2.1 Citizens of the biosphere agree that their requests (for growth, transformation, repairs, etc) be submitted to the influence of the chemical stimuli of the multitude.

2.2 The protocol for exchanges between citizens and the biostructure is freely renewable. It is cancelled if the citizen leaves.

2.3 All citizens are ipso facto owners.

2.4 Rules [1] to [8] apply to everyone as long as they reside in the biosphere.

2.5 For operating instructions and departure procedures, see [6] and [Processes].

3 Self-Alienation

3.0 Citizens agree to become part of a particular social body so as to share physiological information.

3.1 These prepsychic stimuli constitute the second type of inputs, ie internal.

3.1.1 These stimuli arising from the chemical secretions of the multitude of bodies affect the construction logic of the Viab. They are the vectors of its shared reality.

3.2 'Harvesting' takes place through the intermediary of nanoreceptors dispersed throughout the confines of the biostructure and inhaled by the citizens. The functioning of these chemical receptors is described in [Processes].

3.2.1 Their life span is 24 hours. Once this timeframe is over they automatically deactivate and are eliminated by the organism.

3.2.2 The anonymity of chemical data is a general principle.

3.3 Visitors to the biostructure disturb its equilibrium by the mere fact of entering its atmosphere.

3.4 Biostructure citizens are agents making up a reticular mode of political organisation. The resulting unstable equilibrium produces a social mode for which the neighbourhood protocol is both a precondition and a movement.

3.5 The induced behaviour is comparable to a kind of collective intelligence called swarm intelligence. See [Processes].

3.6 The chemical interface with citizens, ie the Viab, infuses, amalgamates and contractualises this political biochemistry.

4 Biopolitics

4.0 The social structure conforms to the territorial structure.

4.1 Creative individualism is a general principle.

4.2 Cohabitation is not based on static principles, but rather on a constant interaction between citizens, non-citizens and the biostructure.

4.3 No one may oppose the arrival of a new citizen and the resulting growth.
This is a general principle.

4.3.1 In the same way, no one may oppose the voluntary departure of a citizen, or invoke a protocol rule against a citizen or a group to demand their departure.

4.4 Each citizen is free to choose their degree of participation and involvement in the life and growth of the biostructure.

4.5 Citizens have access to the data that condition the evolution of the biostructure in all its social aspects. They may propose a modification on the local, meta-local or overall level, and submit it to the multitude by means of the electronic networks running throughout the structure.

4.5.1 Accessing the data means interacting with the structure and being statistically recorded.

4.5.1.2 There are no preconditions for access to the database.

4.5.1.2 The database is a reactive interface: it serves simultaneously as a databank of all entered proposals, a receptor of individual feedback and space where the induced growth can be visualised.

4.5.2 The resulting ensemble of feedback is transmitted to the Viab.

4.5.3 This ensemble constitutes the city's morphological script.

4.6 Individual proposals via the networks can be made at any time. They are purely voluntary and not occasioned by any predetermined programme.

4.6.1 In any proposal, the elements of a situation are brought together on an experimental basis – proposals are speculative tools.

4.6.2 A proposal may be submitted anonymously via the biostructure network.
The collection of individual feedback in electronic form is a general principle.

4.6.3 A proposal is an operative tool. It can only be applied dynamically.
This makes the movement – social experience – a precondition.

4.6.4 A proposal is also a biopolitical tool. It cannot be formulated in a way that implies a delegation of political power in any form.
This is a general principle.

4.7 The collection of feedback makes it possible both to judge the pertinence of the proposal and to call for its adoption or rejection. However, approval or disapproval are not the only possible results in this mechanism. The absence of feedback by more than a third of all citizens renders the proposal null and void.

4.7.1 Nevertheless, no proposal can be permanently rejected. Its reformulation is considered a legitimate renegotiation with the biostructure.

4.8 Any proposal may be presented in two forms simultaneously: one constitutive and permanent, the other experimental and temporary.

4.8.1 Any proposal dismissed in its constitutive version but temporarily approved can be applied on an experimental basis for a period to be defined in the proposal itself. The biostructure is to be consulted again at the end of the experiment.

4.8.2 A group of citizens may choose the manner in which to put an approved experiment into practice. By definition, this will require specific growth.

4.8.3 In this case and only in this case, the experiment and the rhizomes thus generated can be rejected only by the residents of these rhizomes.

4.8.3.1 The preceding is valid as long as these rhizomes do not overturn any general principles.

4.8.3.2 The concept of a rhizome extends beyond its physical existence.

4.9 Because of the social and territorial modifications implied in any proposal challenging one of the basic principles, in order to be adopted (see Open Source [5.2.1]) such a proposal must be reapproved on two occasions, and stated the same way as the original proposal.

4.10 To be approved, a proposal must be shared by a relative localised majority at a time (t).

4.10.1 A relative localised majority is comprised of a group of n citizens living contiguously.

4.10.2 The structure as a whole as well as all of its subgroups are by definition sets of relative localised majorities.

5 Open Source

5.0 Open source is a political and geographic tool.

5.0.1 To recapitulate, the Viab's construction behaviour is generated by a growth algorithm which itself is the result of the miscibility of the two inputs: the chemical and the electronic. See [Entropies].

5.1 All citizens may access the source code upon establishing residence in the biostructure. The source code contains the operating rules: the growth process and the transactional rules. General principles can only be modified under the restrictive conditions defined in point [4.9].

5.1.1 The accessibility of the Viab's source code makes it possible to avoid the implicit pitfalls entailed by its very existence. See [Anomalies].

5.1.2 The modification of the source code within the framework of transactions provided for requires an e-proposal. The implementation of the code modifications thus decided is the only way the Viab is to be reprogrammed.

5.1.3 All operating rules, no matter what kind, can only be understood as variables (environmental, social and construction) modifiable via collective proposals. They are approved electronically and chemically perturbed – see [Self-Alienation].

5.2 Any reprogramming of the Viab that violates this principle or one of the general principles challenges the very structure of society.

5.2.1 If this hypothetical step is taken, the Viab ceases to function in terms of construction and repairs. It becomes deactivated, a residue of the structure.

5.2.2 Nevertheless, following a prolonged deactivation the citizens may reinitialise the Viab's parameters. By exercising this option they return to the neighbourhood protocol 'I've heard about'.

Resultant Schemas

6 Uses

6.1 The dimensions of the structures and their growth along X-Y-Z coordinates depend directly on their localisation and the structural limits of the arborescences.

6.2 A new citizen may adopt one of two residence modes:
– Entropic, which consists of negotiating growth with the structure.
– Nomadic, which consists of borrowing an abandoned cell.
In both cases, the Viab is to carry out the transformations.

6.3 The economic transaction production/transformation takes place through the purchase of a 'time credit' allowing the utilisation of the Viab.

6.3.1 A time credit may be acquired in exchange for induced services, the latter being a production mode of transaction contractualised with the biostructure.

6.4 All citizens are obligated to develop a three-storey habitable space comprising an underground cellar and an attic above the ground floor, no matter how small. Flat, single-storey residences are prohibited. This is a general rule.

6.5 The first phase of residence is nomadic. A cell is developed using a habitability kit. This includes, among other things, a light polymerisable envelope that adapts to the morphological configuration of the empty cell. See [Processes].

6.6 Citizens are completely free to modify, transform or adapt this initial envelope or even to solidify it with the material of their choice. Note that only vertical walls are permanent. The Viab can modify and perforate horizontal structures (ceilings and floors).

6.7 Any use of these cells is allowed, for private or public use or services.

6.8 The transformation of a residence for a different use is negotiable with the adjoining cells. A new mini-neighbourhood protocol is drawn up.

6.8.1 This mini-neighbourhood protocol serves to define the ensemble of shared sensorial elements. The duration of the validity of this contract depends on the effective and corporal presence of the signatory parties.

6.9 When they leave a cell, citizens are obligated to return it to its original state, or in other words to destroy all of the permanent structures they have erected during their residence. An explicit agreement signed by the new resident of a transformed cell derogates this requirement.

7 Scripts

To recapitulate, the structure's morphogenesis is driven by collectively reprogrammable Viabs. Thus the details of the construction algorithm are only provisionally valid.

7.1 The Viab's general principle is structural maintenance.

7.1.1 The Viab infers local structural constraints from the data furnished by the information network that runs through the biostructure.

7.1.2 A structural inability to respond to a request leads the Viab to emit (and possibly itself process) a request for supporting growth.

7.1.3 Available natural light is taken into account, as is power transmission, in the processes of growth by local aggregation and secretion. Growth is particularly facilitated in the structure's convex regions and density is limited by diminishing energy. See [Processes].

7.2 The algorithm of the Viab's movements is described in terms of two levels of abstraction of the reticular structure: wire frame representation and its combinatoric graphing.

7.3 Citizens' requests for growth or maintenance and requests for structural reinforcement (support) originated by the Viab are spatialised by the electronic network. Emitted in one place, they are distributed along the topology of the reticular structure in a gradient whose intensity grows over time.

7.3.1 The Viab acquires requests through these intensity gradients transposed into the pre-existing combinatoric graph of the neighbourhood.

7.4 The primacy of structural maintenance leads the Viab to constantly inspect the structure. The gradients linked to requests and the chemical stimuli respectively act as drift factors and disturbances in this sweep.

7.4.1 The Viab's current technological limitations make a phased movement algorithm necessary. During this movement, the Viab uses a virtual Ariadne's thread anchored in a base point in the biostructure. See [Processes].

7.4.2 The impossibility of even a relatively short-term plan introduces an aleatory element into the Viab's algorithm for spontaneous movement.

7.4.3 The Viab's regular coverage of the entire structure is ensured not despite, but because of, this aleatory element in the movement algorithm. See [Processes].

8 Anomalies

8.0 The Viab is directly affected by the vibrations produced by the superimposition of two types of stimuli. See [Entropies].

8.0.1 Consequently, their heterogeneous combination disturbs the construction algorithm and engenders topological, aesthetic and structural disturbances.

8.0.2 These aberrations, deviations and hybridations, the disorders generated by the Viab's morphological speculations, are intrinsic to its operation.

8.1 There are several types of morphological pathologies:
– Malformations due to deficiencies, cysts, cankers, protuberances, occlusions, etc.
– Degeneration due to necrosis, erosion, fissures, disaggregation, etc.

8.2 These malformations modify the nature of the constructed secretions and alter the definition of familiar geographies.

8.2. Nevertheless, the only malformations the Viab seeks to repair or deprogramme are those that endanger the stability of all or a part of the biostructure.

8.3 Any other physical or aesthetic deformation is to be considered a result of the neighbourhood protocol.

Processes

Accretion n.m. -1. Growth of a region through the inflow and deposit of material. The biostructure's growth is also similar to the polyptych growth of coral.

Biotropism n. (from the Greek *tropos*, direction) -1. Spatially oriented growth among stationary plants and animals under the influence of exterior stimulus (biological, organic or chemical). -2. Intrinsic characteristic of 'I've heard about'.

Contour Crafting (CC) n. -1. A computer-driven construction method that is a mega-scale 3-D printing technology invented by Behrokh Khoshnevis at the University of Southern California. This process of computer-driven construction or, more precisely, secretion, uses an injection nozzle to simultaneously carry out the formwork and the pouring of the walls.

Entropy n. (physics) -1. Magnitude that makes it possible to measure the degree of disorder in a system.

Nanoreceptors n. (physics, from nanos: $1nm = 10^{-9} m$) -1. Nanoparticles (NP) used to capture and detect the presence of a chemical substance in a particular atmosphere. -2A. Nanoreceptors can be inhaled, making it possible to 'sniff' the chemical state of the human body. -2B. Functioning: like pollens, they are concentrated in the bronchia and attach themselves to the blood vessels. This location makes it possible for them to detect traces of stress hormones (hydrocortisone) carried by the haemoglobin. As soon as they come into contact with this substance, the phospholipidic membrane of the NP dissolves and releases several molecules, including formaldehyde ($H2CO$) in a gaseous state. The molecules rejected by the respiratory tract are detected using cavity ring-down spectroscopy (CRDS). This is a method of optical analysis using laser beams programmed to a particular frequency, making it possible to measure the density of airborne molecules. The wavelength used for the detection of formaldehyde is around 350 nanometres. -3. Consequently, the nanoreceptors keep the Viabs informed about the ambient stress level.

Prepsychism n. -1. Preverbal state of consciousness of an individual in which the self has no importance, a body that does not think but senses its surroundings and lets itself change to let itself be touched and felt, to 'become porous to every breath'. By extension, the necessary condition for chemically sharing, and rereading the biochemical citizen through nanoreceptors in the 'I've heard about' structure.

Swarm intelligence n. -1. Term designating a form of behaviour characterised by the absence of central control or overall architecture. By extension, the 'local growth stimuli' produced by individual requests for the extension of the structure and the chemical data which together determine the actual construction work performed by each Viab. These growth stimuli are the result of individual behaviours, determined at the local level (particularly by negotiations between next-door neighbours and nanoreceptors).

Viab n. (Contraction of variability-viability) -1A. A reactive and autonomous construction machine employing secretion. Developed for the first biostructure, the Viab launches a robotic algorithm that allows it to build architectural structures based on the principles of indeterminacy. Its open-source programming makes it permeable to external inputs. Its basic script defines protocols for action, movement and all sorts of constraints, but also entirely integrates environmental variables that could affect its primary function. -1B. An explanation of its functioning: the support rail on which it moves, similar to a crane track, is secreted by the Viab itself. Articulated pneumatic arms move the secretion heads. During pouring the assembly is rigidified as the heads lock into the structure to be extended. The formwork is generated using a telescopic arm with a nozzle at the end. This system incorporates the variation between the diameters of the various structural sections. Pouring is carried out simply by filling this shell. As the machine advances the secretion head moves by the alternate inflation and deflation of three pneumatic valves. At the end of a particular construction phase, the articulated arm retracts into the Viab. The latter can move along the rail to reach a future growth zone. ⌂

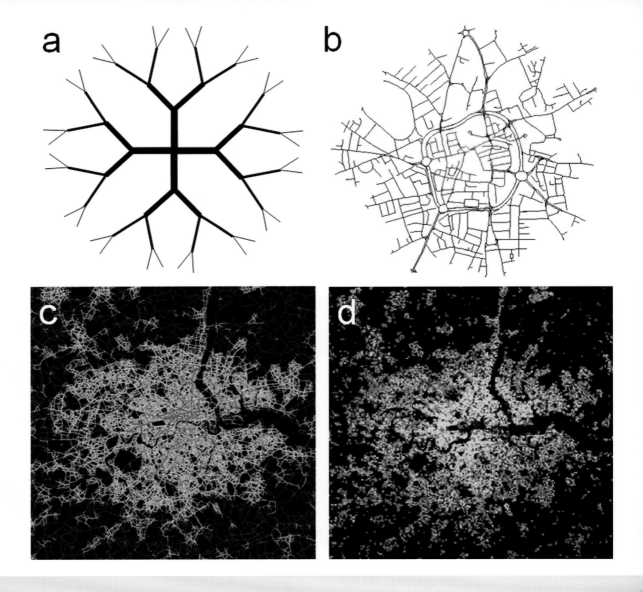

A Digital Breeder for Designing Cities

The idea that inspired designs mirror processes of biological evolution is fast gaining ground as we learn more about how complex systems such as cities function. **Michael Batty** illustrates how cities can now be grown in 'digital laboratories' and, by imposing realistic constraints on their form, begin to breed 'good designs' that emerge from continual feedbacks that reinforce the best and iron out the worst.

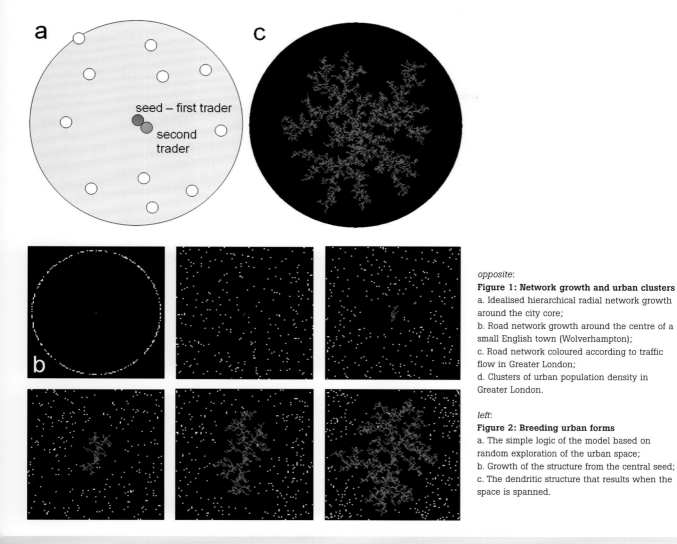

opposite:

Figure 1: Network growth and urban clusters
a. Idealised hierarchical radial network growth around the city core;
b. Road network growth around the centre of a small English town (Wolverhampton);
c. Road network coloured according to traffic flow in Greater London;
d. Clusters of urban population density in Greater London.

left:

Figure 2: Breeding urban forms
a. The simple logic of the model based on random exploration of the urban space;
b. Growth of the structure from the central seed;
c. The dendritic structure that results when the space is spanned.

This year marks the 200th anniversary of the birth of Charles Darwin and the 150th anniversary of his book *On the Origin of Species,* which changed the world. In timely fashion, Darwin's fundamental message that life proceeds through a natural selection that slowly but surely preserves the fittest among the population and destroys the rest, appears increasingly attractive in explaining the growth dynamics of a variety of non-biological organisations such as cities. Such selection proceeds in very small steps that most now agree take place at the genetic level, with the result that those organisms that survive are very well adapted to their environment and to each other. In analogous fashion, cities are one of the best exemplars of how well-adapted designs emerge from what appear to be countless uncoordinated decisions generated from the bottom up that produce order on all scales. This emergence of order is the hallmark of complex systems, and it is hardly surprising that with the growth of digital computation it is now possible to

simulate such evolutionary processes, thereby suggesting how 'good designs' might emerge among a universe of possible designs.

If good urban designs can be grown by manipulating this kind of complexity, then this promises to provide a much more sensitive, less intrusive way of managing our environments than the blunt instruments that have hitherto characterised planning. City design should thus ascribe to Darwin's message that it is small changes intelligently identified in the city fabric, rather than massive, monumental plans, that lead to more successful, liveable and certainly more sustainable environments. Christopher Alexander continues to preach this message, as did Jane Jacobs,[1] but it has been a long time in coming.

In the last 20 years, it has become clear that cities, far from being messy, disorganised forms, have rather well-defined spatial structures. Order and pattern appear on all scales, with urban activities forming clusters of different sizes. These clusters are supported by networks which transport energy to sustain them and which fill space efficiently as tree-like hierarchies. These represent the most parsimonious ways of delivering energy to population clusters that diffuse to take the greatest advantage of the space around them. Figure 1 shows a sample of real

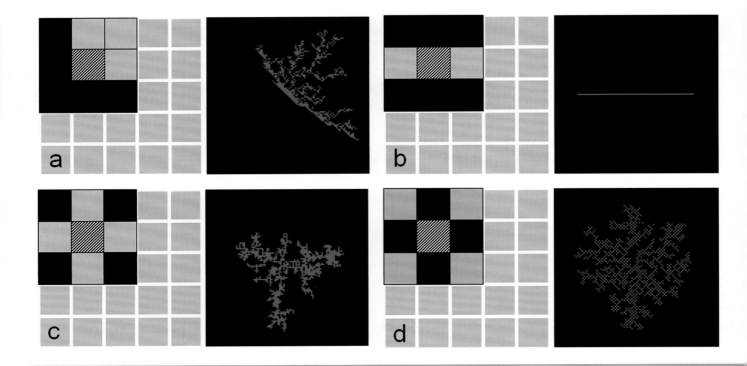

and idealised networks and clusters of urban development based on dendritic forms that fill space in such a way that the city remains connected. These structures are fractals, objects which are self-similar at successive scales, forming clusters whose distribution follows scaling or power laws according to a strict hierarchy and frequency of sizes. The most complete examples of organic order occur in cities with no central planning, such as those developed in the medieval period in Europe[2] and, more recently, in the rapidly developing cities of the Third World.

Growing city shapes, such as those in Figure 1, from the bottom up in digital laboratories requires clear rules to be specified that determine how agents locate with respect to one another. As a minimum, these rules must reflect two very basic forces: first, that people aggregate in cities to realise scale economies of agglomeration, which means that people should always be connected to one another; and second, that people should be able to live with as much space around them as possible. These two forces compete and contradict each other: the first leads to centripetal growth, the second to centrifugal. Now imagine a uniform homogeneous plain and a trader who decides to settle at the intersection of a track and a river where the land is fertile and flat. If another trader happens, by chance, to find the trader who has settled, that trader also decides to settle there. In the wider hinterland, a certain proportion of traders will find the

settlement with a certain probability. Given enough time and enough traders, the settlement will grow, but how?

A schematic of the location process is demonstrated in Figure 2a. The individuals who seek to settle are arranged around a circle well outside the location of the settlement, the centre of which is the red solid dot where the original trader locates. Each individual is a solid white dot who begins to search for the 'city' – the red dot – via a random walk. If they find a cell adjacent to the red dot, they settle, turn 'red' and no longer move. Another white dot is launched somewhere in the hinterland and the process continues with many white dots searching for the city of red dots. The city builds up, not as a compact mass, but as a dendritic structure, based on the way the two principles of proximity and space interact. The result is surprising in that order emerges from the bottom up, with the actual shape dependent on a sequence of incremental, randomly determined decisions. The structure that emerges is path dependent and thus 'history counts'. Figure 2b shows the growth path where the final structure in Figure 2c is not a compact mass with a dimension of 2 or a linear city with a dimension of 1, but a pure dendrite, a fractal, with a fractional dimension of about 1.7.

To breed new designs, these rules need to be manipulated to reflect the principles for growth. They reflect a genetic code in that they tell the location how to respond to the agent and vice versa, which is accomplished by forming rules that pertain to the vicinity or neighbourhood of each location in question. These rules encode any relevant information and, in the case of the species of 'agents' in Figure 2, they consist of simply telling the agent to fix its location if

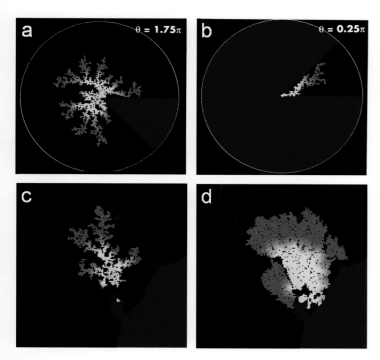

opposite:

Figure 3: Configuring the rules that generate urban morphology by cellular automata
a. Rules that orientate the city to the northeast;
b. Rules that force the morphology into a linear city destroying the variety of form;
c. Rules that keep development compact and linear;
d. Rules that keep development compact and sparse.

left:

Figure 4: Growing cities in a physically restricted container
a. Around a river estuary;
b. On a spit of headland;
c. Cardiff under the standard diffusion–limited aggregation growth model;
d. Cardiff under a set of rules that reinforce compactness.

another agent has already settled in its neighbourhood. The model is a cellular automaton where the cells (locations) in the neighbourhood determine what happens to the cell in question. Figure 3 illustrates what happens when the rules are changed by excluding some cells from consideration (shown in black in each of the cellular templates with the resultant breed alongside).

Thus linear cities can be generated only where linearly adjacent cells can be developed or cities skewed in orientation due to climatic influences which restrict development to, for example, their windward side and so on. The general idea is to specify rules that are both realistic and optimal, that do not break the process of ordinary decision-making but mutate and interact to produce good designs. Figure 4 suggests 'containers' can be defined in which such breeding takes place and which mirror the topography of both ideal cities and real cities, such as Cardiff. Actual cities evolve towards designs that are at least sustainable and, to some degree, workable, and thus the starting point should always be the rules that generate real cities. The challenge lies in defining changes to these rules that improve the workings of real cities by meeting goals pertaining to flows, densities and economies of agglomeration.

The digital tools used to generate cities in this manner and to breed different urban forms are now widely available as packages that allow cellular systems (incorporating principles of cellular automata) and agent-based models to be constructed. Starlogo from MIT's Media Lab and its Web equivalent, Netlogo, are the most generic, but more specific packages such as RePast for agent-based models are also available, all as freeware or open source.[3] What is required now is further experimentation with these kinds of models by others who are able to fashion such systems to meet different constraints and objectives, thus generating as wide an array of possible city forms as can be imagined. ⌂

Notes
1. The organic analogy between design, buildings and cities was first formally presented by Jane Jacobs in her book *The Death and Life of Great American Cities,* Random House (New York), 1961, and at much the same time by Christopher Alexander in his *Notes of the Synthesis of Form,* Harvard University Press (Cambridge, MA), 1964. Alexander's recent magnum opus, *The Nature of Order,* CES Publishing (Berkeley, CA), 2004, takes these ideas much further.
2. Excellent examples of cities in history that display the kind of organic order which is a consequence of growth from the bottom up are contained in Spiro Kostof's *The City Shaped: Urban Patterns and Meanings Through History,* WW Norton & Co Inc (New York), 1993. An outline of cities as fractals is included in Michael Batty and Paul Longley, 'The Fractal City', *Architectural Design,* 67 (9–10), 1977, pp 74–83, while the book by the same authors, *Fractal Cities,* Academic Press (San Diego, CA), 1994, deals with the mechanics of how to construct these models (see http://www.fractalcities.org/). Extensions to the models are illustrated in Michael Batty, *Cities and Complexity,* MIT Press (Cambridge, MA), 2005, and a more detailed discussion of the cellular automata methods used to breed cities in this way can be found online in *Cluster Magazine* at http://www.cluster.eu/v2/editions/batty/.
3. Starlogo software for any platform can be downloaded from http://education.mit.edu/starlogo/, and Netlogo from http://ccl.northwestern.edu/netlogo/. A good source for agent-based modelling software including RePast is Andrew Crooks's blog http://gisagents.blogspot.com/.

The Limits of Urban

An Interview with Manuel DeLanda

What is the potential for applying digital simulation for research in urban planning and development? **Neil Leach** pursues this question with influential 'street philosopher', one-time programmer and professor Manuel DeLanda.

Simulation

Guilherme Ressel, Digital Favelas, Dessau Institute of Architecture (tutor: Neil Leach), Germany, 2006
This project is scripted using a formal vocabulary derived from the logic of actual *favelas* from Brazil to generate a pattern of spontaneous urban growth which progressively colonises the landscape.

Manuel DeLanda has exerted an enormous impact on architectural culture. For several years now the self-styled 'street philosopher' has been teaching at some of the world's leading schools of architecture. He is the author of a number of highly influential books, including his critically acclaimed volume on urban growth patterns, *A Thousand Years of Non-Linear History*.[1] However, he also has a background as a programmer, and has written numerous high-profile articles about architecture and digital design, such as 'Deleuze and the Use of the Genetic Algorithm in Architecture'.[2] It was therefore pertinent to ask him whether he has made any connections between his interest in digital simulation and his research into urban planning.

'On one hand, some of the earliest applications of far-from equilibrium thermodynamics and nonlinear dynamics to social science were simulations of urban growth patterns, as in the work of Peter Allen. Those early simulations were very influential in my work, partly because those two areas of physics are crucial to theories of self-organisation. On the other hand, despite my early interest in artificial intelligence, it is only now that I am mastering the technical details of simulations (from cellular automata and genetic algorithms to multi-agent systems) to write my new book, technical details that are necessary to any serious approach to urban dynamics. Unfortunately, the new book had to stop with a chapter on pyramid building in Egypt, in which the simulations are applied to institutional organisations not cities. So a full encounter between digital simulations and urban settlements in my work will have to wait for the future.'

Nonetheless, DeLanda does have some interesting observations to offer on the potential of using digital simulations for urban settlements. We need to distinguish between the various forms of simulation. For DeLanda there are two types: continuous and discrete. 'Continuous urban simulations use differential equations to capture the rate of growth of a given city (as a function of other rates, like immigration rates, birth and death rates of citizens, rates of energy consumption) or to capture rates of urbanisation over entire regions. In computers the continuous differential equations must in fact be "discretised" over a space-time grid of a given resolution, but their continuous nature is recovered as the spatial distances and temporal intervals become smaller.'

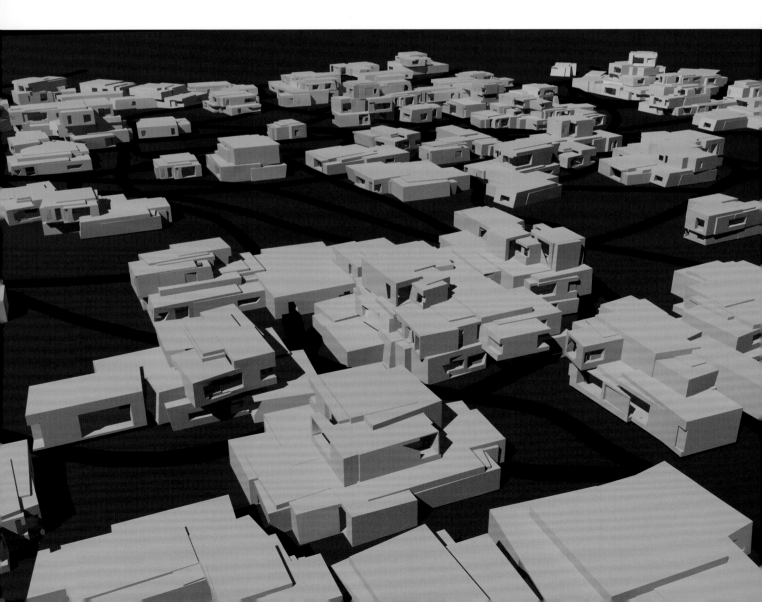

Pascal Müller, CityEngine, Procedural Inc, 2008
left: CityEngine is a commercially available software program that uses procedural modelling to generate rapid simulations of urban environments.

Guilherme Ressel, Digital Favelas, Dessau Institute of Architecture (tutor: Neil Leach), Germany, 2006
opposite: A range of possible architectural solutions is placed on the available terrain, based on algorithms that evaluate the topography and existing amenities in the surrounding area. During this process the design is tested continuously by artificial intelligence that simulates pedestrian movements generating a self-organising process of urban landscape formation.

But there are also fully discrete models of urban simulation in which one attempts to derive those rates of growth from the bottom up. 'These are called "multi-agent" systems, and consist of discrete entities (agents) whose behaviour is specified by rules (and hence it is not emergent) but which can interact with each other and produce emergent effects from these interactions. In a given simulation the trick is to find the level of resolution for the agents. Are they supposed to be individual persons? Or individual communities, such as those inhabiting specific neighbourhoods? Or individual organisations, like schools, hospitals, government agencies, factories? In this second kind of simulation the most important thing is to be clear as to the relations between agents at different scales.'

In his work, DeLanda treats these as relations of part to whole. 'Persons are the component parts of communities and organisations; communities the component parts of social justice movements and of social classes; and organisations the component parts of industrial networks and federal governments. Cities, in turn, are the physical locales in which those entities perform their day-to-day activities, and they themselves display a nested set of part-to-whole relations: individual buildings, individual neighbourhoods and districts, and so on. Thus, before applying multi-agent simulations one must be clear about these nested sets in which wholes at one scale are the parts of wholes at the next scale.'

This brings us to the question of buildings themselves. DeLanda mentions buildings in the context of 'physical locales'. He also mentions one specific building type: the pyramid. But in his work the pyramids are read in terms of the organisational structure of their building processes, rather than in terms of their physical form. What relevance – if any – would the actual form of buildings have within his frame of reference?

'Unfortunately I do not have a good answer to this question because I have never written anything about design, architectural or otherwise. But the analysis of locales in which practices are conducted (buildings, neighbourhoods, cities) does relate to form in two different ways. First of all, they are all typically divided into regions (rooms with different functions, such as kitchens, bedrooms, living rooms, or buildings with different functions, like churches, pubs, offices, factories, or neighbourhoods with different functions – residential, industrial, governmental) and these regions must be accessible from one another; that is, there must be a certain connectivity (by doors and hallways, streets and alleys, mass transportation and so on).

'Both the regionalisation of buildings and their connectivity have a history, which I have only superficially explored. The main example I use comes from Fernand Braudel who claims that prior to the 18th century the connectivity of French residential buildings was such that servants had to walk through the master bedroom to reach other rooms. Then a change occurred in the connectivity, isolating the master bedroom and therefore affording its occupants privacy for the first time.'

If we were to strip away any notion of aesthetics from our understanding of design, and treat the fabric of the city as a mineralisation of the human exoskeleton, as the form that is generated in response to complex social, cultural, economic, geographic and other factors, as DeLanda had suggested in *A Thousand Years of Non-Linear History*, might this nonetheless give us something to work with?

'In that book I approached the subject in terms of the collective unintended consequences of intentional action. These consequences are much more obvious in the case of decentralised decision-making than in the centralised case. I used as my extreme examples the medieval core of Venice, whose labyrinthine structure was the unintended product of many decentralised personal decisions, and Versailles, a city planned to the last detail by centralised decision-makers in the French government. Clearly, most cities (or even different parts of a city) are a combination of these two extremes. And different periods of history display different combinations in which one or the other of the two extremes predominate. I have in mind here the period starting after the Thirty Years War, when the concept of national sovereignty first appeared in a peace treaty (in effect signalling the birth of international law). This age also marked the end of the city-state, the final absorption of cities into larger territories, and the transformation of former regional capitals into national capitals, many of which were then submitted to intense planning and reorganisation.'

Before we can generate buildings themselves, we must model the decision-making processes that give rise to them.

However, for DeLanda digital simulations of these processes need to be quite complex. 'To simulate these processes we need multi-agent systems that are more elaborate than, say, those used in the program Sugarscape, in which agents have a metabolism (they must gather or trade resources to survive) and move around in space creating stable settlements. Yet they hardly make any decisions (they follow rules). So we need something like the type of agent known as Belief-Desire-Intention agents, who can not only make decisions based on their beliefs and desires, but also attribute to others such intentional states and use those attributions to modify their own decisions. With these agents, and some way of representing authority structures so that we can have binding centralised decisions, we could test the collective effect of many of them on the form of neighbourhoods or even entire cities.'

It is important here to see these agents not as abstract entities that embody the collective intelligence of an entire society, but as individuals or groups as such. 'There is no such thing as the collective intelligence of an entire society. I wrote my last book (*A New Philosophy of Society*) precisely to demolish that idea once and for all. Rather, agency must be attributed to concrete, singular, individual entities existing at many levels of scale:

persons are agents, but so are communities (when they form coalitions in social justice movements, for example). Institutional organisations too are agents, as are assemblages of such organisations, like industrial networks or federal governments.'

When using multi-agent simulations, we must first establish at what scale we will be modelling a given phenomenon. 'For example, when discussing trade between two cities, does it make a difference what individual persons carried out the trade? (Yes, if we are modelling very short timescales.) Or is it the sustained regularity and volume of trade over many decades that influenced urban form? In the case of planning bureaucracies the same question emerges. In the case of the planning of Versailles we must include the agency of Colbert, since he was personally instrumental in the making of many decisions. In other examples, the actual bosses of a bureaucracy do not matter: the same outcome would have occurred regardless of the current leader. The point is that we cannot tell a priori what level of agency is the most important without considering actual historical situations.'

DeLanda places great emphasis on 'decision-making agents'. In practice, however, many urban interventions are based on rules – zoning laws, building codes and regulations, rights of light and so on. And, if we are to believe Christopher Alexander, human beings always favour a form of 'pattern language'. Some fairly sophisticated rule-based engines for simulating urban growth, such as CityEngine, have been developed for the gaming industry. So what does DeLanda see as being the limitations of these engines in modelling the specificities of urban form?

Krassimir Krastev and Fabiano Friedrich, Urbanoids, Budapest, Dessau Institute of Architecture (tutor: Neil Leach), Germany, 2005
Two interconnected computer programs were here developed in order to explore the possibilities of re-establishing the unique character of an inner-city site in Budapest: a pedestrian movement simulation and a genetic algorithm. Guided by basic artificial intelligence, computer-simulated characters explore the site looking for targets. The paths created are recorded and evaluated according to their intensity of use. The busiest pathways become attractors for new retail spaces.

A genetic algorithm is utilised to generate the distribution of these retail spaces. Their new distribution at ground-floor level means new attractors for pedestrians. Optimal profiles for the buildings are bred, based on space syntax logic of visibilities and sun-path diagrams.

'Rule-guided behaviour is a standard approach in simulations of populations of agents. But our brains are not rule-based: neural network simulations work exclusively with pattern recognition and pattern completion, and do not store explicit representations, but only a pattern of strengths in their synapses, a pattern capable of recreating the original pattern of excitation when stimulated. It is the pattern of excitation that acts as a kind of implicit, distributed representation.

'On the other hand, there is no need to put neural nets into agents in every simulation. The behaviour of an agent using neural nets seems from the outside to be rule-driven, so for some purposes we can replace them with explicit rules. And then, of course, there are institutional norms and regulations that act as external constraints on behaviour. These can be simulated simply by adding explicit constraints to agents, but if what we want to do is to analyse how building practices co-evolve with regulations, then the latter need to be modelled in more detail.

'Government organisations (bureaucratic agencies) must be added to the simulations as institutional agents, their authority (and the authority of their edicts) modelled both in terms of their legitimacy (does it derive from tradition, or from their proven track record?) and the

means of their enforcement. As legitimacy changes and as enforcement practices evolve, the rules themselves change.

'So it is a matter of what timescales we are simulating: for the timescale typical of the duration of a construction project (say, a few years) norms and regulations can be modelled as given and unchanging; for longer timescales (say, the evolution of land-use succession in a city over many decades), the norms themselves must be allowed to change.'

Amid the rash of recent attempts to explore the potential of generating digital simulations of urban growth, DeLanda offers us some cautionary advice. Before we can generate buildings themselves, we must model the decision-making processes that give rise to them. And in order to do this, we must be able to devise intelligent decision-making agents that can influence others and reflect upon their own decisions. Only then, it would seem, would we be in a position to simulate the growth of actual cities. △

This interview has been compiled from email correspondence between Neil Leach and Manuel DeLanda from October to November 2008.

Notes
1. Manuel DeLanda, *A Thousand Years of Nonlinear History*, Zone Books, Swerve Editions (New York), 1997. See also: DeLanda, *War in the Age of Intelligent Machines*, Zone Books (New York), 1992; DeLanda, *Intensive Science, Virtual Philosophy*, Continuum (New York), 2002; DeLanda, *A New Philosophy of Society*, Continuum (New York), 2006.
2. Manuel DeLanda, 'Deleuze and the Use of the Genetic Algorithm in Architecture', in N Leach (ed), *Designing for a Digital World*, John Wiley & Sons (London), 2002, pp 117–20.

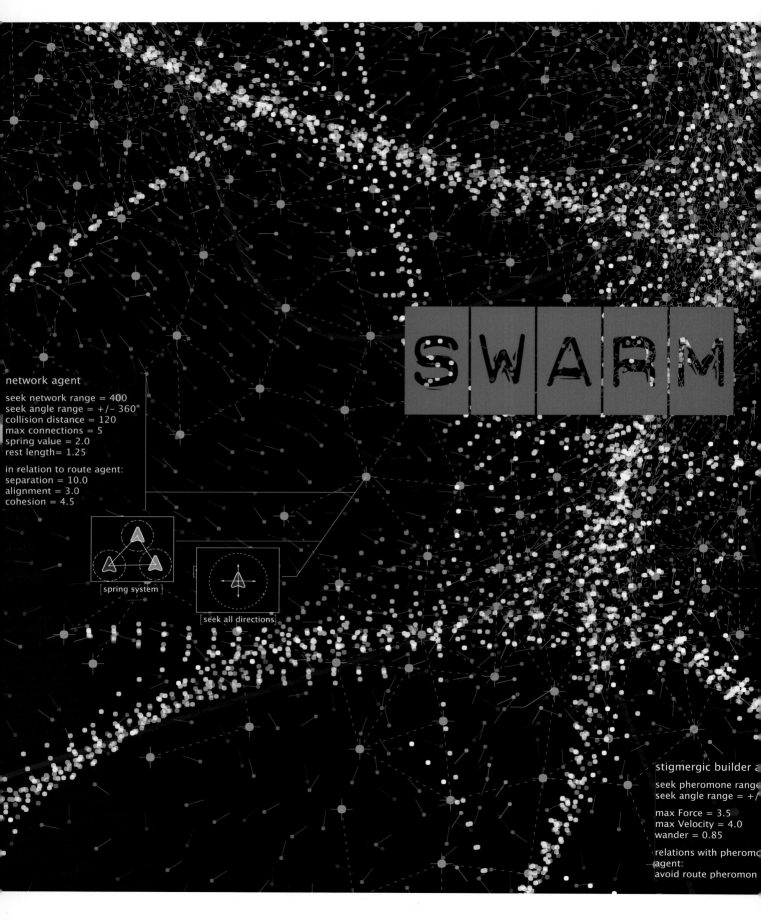

network agent

seek network range = 400
seek angle range = +/− 360°
collision distance = 120
max connections = 5
spring value = 2.0
rest length= 1.25

in relation to route agent:
separation = 10.0
alignment = 3.0
cohesion = 4.5

[spring system]

[seek all directions]

SWARM

stigmergic builder a
seek pheromone rang
seek angle range = +/

max Force = 3.5
max Velocity = 4.0
wander = 0.85

relations with pheromo
agent:
avoid route pheromon

cluster agent

seek network range = 80
seek angle range = +/- 60°

seperation distance = 40.0
alignment = 2.0
cohesion = 5.0

in relation to network agent
seperation distance = 70.0
alignment = 1.0
cohesion = 3.0

[separation]   [cohesion]

[alignment]   [seek]

URBANISM

[seek pheromone]

[emit pheromone]

[seek matter]

[emit matter]

pheromone route agent

seek pheromone range = 100
seek angle range = +/- 25°

max Force = 7.5
max Velocity = 8.0
wander = 0.65

in relation to stigmergic builder:
seek pheromone range = 65

[emit pheromone]

As dense human settlements, cities can be regarded as manifestations of emergent behaviour — not unlike like that of a colony of ants or a flock of birds. **Neil Leach** explores how software programs that display a similar emergent logic to cities might lend themselves to the development of a new computational methodology for modelling urban form.

In his book *Emergence: The Connected Lives of Ants, Cities and Software*, Steven Johnson presents the city as a manifestation of emergence.[1] The city operates as a dynamic, adaptive system, based on interactions with neighbours, informational feedback loops, pattern recognition and indirect control. 'Like any emergent system,' notes Johnson, 'the city is a pattern in time.'[2] Moreover, like any other population composed of a large number of smaller discrete elements, such as colonies of ants, flocks of birds, networks of neurons or even the global economy, it displays a bottom-up collective intelligence that is more sophisticated than the behaviour of its parts. In short, the city operates through a form of 'swarm intelligence'.

Aerial view of Rocinha *favela*, a large slum on the hills behind Copacabana in Rio de Janeiro, Brazil.

'Emergence' has become a highly popular term in recent architectural discourse, but it is worth recalling that the term itself does not necessarily refer to contemporary design issues.[3] On the contrary, it could be argued that emergence could be viewed most clearly in traditional urban formations. For it is precisely the less self-conscious forms of urban aggregation that characterise the development of traditional settlements, from medieval villages to Chinese *hutongs* or Brazilian *favelas*, that fit best the simple rules of emergence, such as 'ignorance is useful' or 'pay attention to your neighbours'. These forms of urbanism constitute a relatively homogeneous field of operations, where individual components do not stand out, but conform to the pervasive logic of their surrounding environment. In this sense, we might understand emergence as operating within the framework of what Gianni Vattimo calls 'weak thought' (*pensiero debole*).[4] This is not to say that the signature buildings of the contemporary city do not offer examples of emergence. Rather, emergence is most recognisable in the proliferation of architectures of the everyday.[5]

Yet 'emergence' does have a highly contemporary relevance. Importantly, Johnson extends the principle of emergence to the operations of certain software programs. If cities and software programs display a similar emergent logic, how might we make use of digital technologies to model a city? Let us begin with a note of caution: the complexity of material computation within the city far exceeds anything that we might be able to model as yet through digital computation.[6] Nonetheless, it would seem important to address this question, and explore the potential of computational methodology for modelling urban form.

It is clear from the outset that whatever computational methodology is adopted it must itself follow the logic of swarm intelligence. In other words, it needs to exceed the capacities of fractals, L-systems, cellular automata and other systems that operate largely within their own discrete internal logic. Fractals and L-systems are limited for modelling patterns of growth in that they are programmed to behave in a particular way, and in general cannot adjust their behaviour in response to external stimuli.[7] Meanwhile, although cellular automata can respond to their neighbours, they are fixed spatially, and therefore tied to certain underlying grids. What we are looking for, then, is a multi-agent system comprised of intelligent agents interacting with one another and capable of spatial mobility.

Kokkugia, Melbourne Docklands, Melbourne, Australia, 2008
previous spread: The decentralised structure of swarm, or multi-agent, systems changes the nature of hierarchy in urbanism. Hierarchies of scale and intensity are of course imperative to urbanism; however, the swarm logic developed for the Melbourne Docklands flattens the hierarchy within the design process. All elements of the urban fabric are conceived of as possessing agency, enabling them to interact without a sequential design hierarchy; instead the hierarchy of intensities at a macro scale is an emergent outcome of their self-organising operation. As such, urban elements including infrastructure are not a priori, but rather one of many co-dependent systems that self-organise together to generate a mutually resilient organisation.

Kokkugia, Melbourne Docklands, Melbourne, Australia, 2008
below: Agency operates through two main processes within this proposal: first, by using design agents to self-organise urban matter, and second, to encode intelligence into urban elements and topologies. In the first category agents operate to self-organise programme through a process of stigmergic growth. This type of collective behavior is similar to the logic of termite colonies in aggregating matter to form their mounds. The second category of agents works in a similar manner to the processes that govern the self-organisation of slime mould cells into minimal path systems or the collective organisation of ants to create bridges. These urban agents are primarily used to generate infrastructural and circulatory networks.

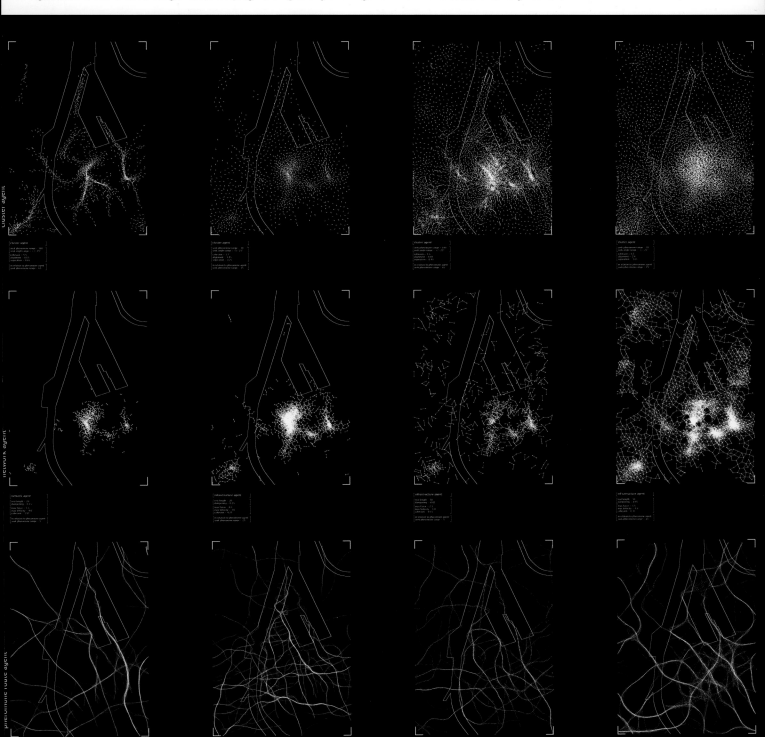

One practice that does use swarm intelligence as a fully bottom-up multi-agent design tool is Kokkugia, a network of young Australian architects operating from New York and London.

Swarm Intelligence

There are a number of ways of modelling swarm intelligence within a computational framework. Manuel DeLanda outlines a model of agent-based behaviour that could be developed to understand the decision-making processes within an actual city.[8] These agents should be seen as concrete, singular individual agents, and not as abstract agents that embody the collective intelligence of an entire society. DeLanda's research to date is based on institutional organisations rather than urban forms of the city, and while he envisages the possibility of a model which uses a system of intelligent agents capable of making their own decisions and of influencing others in their decisions in order to generate urban form in some way, he has yet to develop this model.

The term 'swarm urbanism' has been used fairly extensively within design circles. Often this refers to a form of 'swarm effect', where a grid is morphed parametrically using either digital tools or Frei Otto's 'wet grid' analogue technique.[9] Such techniques, while producing interesting effects, are limited in that they are either topologically fixed (as with a morphodynamic lattice) or base geometrically fixed (as with the wet grid), and cannot make qualitative shifts in form and space outside of these set-ups. The advantage of a genuinely bottom-up emergent system of swarm intelligence where individual agents with embedded intelligence respond to one another is that it offers behavioural translations of topology and geometry that can have radically varied outputs.[10]

One practice that does use swarm intelligence as a fully bottom-up multi-agent design tool is Kokkugia, a network of young Australian architects operating from New York and London.[11] They have deployed this technique at a macro level for a project in the Docklands in Melbourne, an urban redevelopment currently under construction focusing on the extension of the Central Business District into a disued port territory, and have extended it to a micro level with the design of actual buildings, as with their Taipei Performing Arts Centre.

With their swarm urbanism projects, the concern of Kokkugia is not to simulate actual populations (of people or institutions) or their occupation of architecture, but to devise processes operating at much greater levels of abstraction that involve seeding design intent into a set of autonomous design agents which are capable of self-organising into emergent urban forms. They are therefore not interested in mapping the motion of swarming agents to generate an urban plan as a single optimal solution, but rather in developing a flexible system embodying a collective self-organising urban intelligence: 'An application of swarm logic to urbanism enables a shift from notions of the master-plan to that of master-algorithm as an urban design tool. This shift changes the conception of urban design from a sequential set of decisions at reducing scales, to a simultaneous process in which a set of micro or local decisions interact to generate a complex urban system. Rather than designing an urban plan that meets a finite set of criteria, urban imperatives are programmed into a set of agents which are able to self-organise.'[12]

This approach tends to produce a result which – if not reducible to a single steady-state condition – will eventually coalesce into a near-equilibrium, semi-stable state always teetering on the brink of disequilibrium.[13] This allows the system to remain responsive to changing economic, political and social circumstances. Kokkugia therefore sees the urban condition as one of constant flux: 'Our urban design methodology does not seek to find a single optimum solution but rather a dynamically stable state that feeds off the instabilities of the relations that comprise it.'[14]

Rhizomatic Urbanism

One way of taking this approach further, from a theoretical perspective, is to appropriate the notion of the 'rhizome' from Gilles Deleuze and Félix Guattari as an urban planning strategy. In their seminal work, *A Thousand Plateaus*, Deleuze and Guattari seem to offer a theoretical model that resonates closely with the logic of emergence. For example, they refer extensively to multiplicities, to packs of wolves and to the logic of the crowd.[15] Meanwhile, one of the central tenets of their philosophy is 'population thinking' – the idea that 'the population not the individual is *the matrix for the production of form*.'[16] Moreover, they touch upon the logic of the city itself as a space of flows. Deleuze and Guattari describe the town/city as a network, a phenomenon of transconsistency, that 'exists only as a function of circulation, and of circuits'.[17] For cities and towns themselves must be understood as amalgams of 'processes', as spaces of vectorial flows that 'adjust' to differing inputs and impulses, like some self-regulating system.[18]

Kokkugia, Melbourne Docklands, Melbourne, Australia, 2008
The Melbourne Docklands proposal is an investigation into an urban design methodology based on the emergent capacities of swarm intelligence. This speculative project posits a further intensification of the masterplan in a manner that transforms its urban typology through the concept of urbanism as an ecosystem.

Deleuze and Guattari use the interaction between a wasp and an orchid to illustrate their concept of the rhizome. The example is a familiar enough one – of an insect being attracted to a plant, and thereby serving to cross-pollinate that plant.[19] The wasp is of course being 'housed' by the orchid, thereby giving the description a certain architectural relevance. But what interests Deleuze and Guattari most of all is the interaction between wasp and orchid. The orchid has developed attributes that attract the wasp, but so too the wasp has developed a pattern of behaviour that serves the orchid. As Deleuze and Guattari observe, wasp and orchid enter into a mutual reciprocity, such that the wasp has adapted to the orchid, no less than the orchid has adapted to the wasp. Deleuze and Guattari refer to this as a form of mutual 'becoming'. The wasp becomes like the orchid, and the orchid becomes like the wasp, or – more precisely – the wasp has evolved in response to the orchid, just as the orchid has evolved in response to the wasp.

Importantly for Deleuze and Guattari, we must perceive both wasp and orchid in terms of a multiplicity. They form an 'assemblage', an 'acentred multiplicity that is subjected to continuous movement and variation'.[20] As Greg Lynn explains: 'The multiple orchids and wasps unify to form a singular body. This propagating unity is not an enclosed whole, but a multiplicity: the wasps and orchids are simultaneously one and many bodies. What is important is that there is not a pre-existing collective body that was displaced by this parasitic exchange of sexual desire but rather a new stable body is composed from the intricate connections of these previously disparate bodies. Difference is in the service of a fusional multiplicity that produces new stable bodies through incorporations that remain open to further influence by other external forces.'[21]

Deleuze and Guattari describe this process through the concept of the rhizome: 'Wasp and orchid, as heterogeneous elements, form a rhizome.'[22] The logic of the rhizome should be distinguished from that of the tree. As John Marks explains: 'The model of the tree is

hierarchical and centralised, whereas the rhizome is proliferating and serial, functioning by means of the principles of connection and heterogeneity … The rhizome is a multiplicity.'[23] Central to the concept of the rhizome is the principle of 'becoming', of forming a relationship with the other, as in the case of wasp and orchid, where the one deterritorialises the other: 'The wisdom of plants: even when they have roots, there is always an outside where they form a rhizome with something else — with the wind, an animal, human beings (and there is also an aspect under which animals themselves form rhizomes, as do people, etc).'[24] By extension, we could understand the city as forming a rhizome with its inhabitants.

This opens up an intriguing way of understanding the relationship between humans as 'agents' within this system and the fabric of the city as a form of exoskeleton to human operations. We need to distinguish between the city as a site of material composition – as an amalgam of traces of construction – and the city as the site of spatial practices. The former can be read in terms of an accretion of material deposits, and the latter can be read in terms of choreographies of agents whose freedom of movement is constrained by these material deposits. It as though the city is 'formed' by registering the impulses of human occupation, much as the sheets on our beds, for example, record the movements of our bodies through the night. But so, too, the city constrains the possibilities of human movement through its very physicality. There is, therefore, in Deleuzian terms, a form of reciprocal presupposition between city and occupants. The city modifies its occupants, no less than the occupants modify the city. Over time the fabric of the city evolves through interaction with its inhabitants.

The task of design therefore would be to anticipate what would have evolved over time from the interaction between inhabitants and city. If we adopt the notion of 'scenario planning' that envisages the potential choreographies of use within a particular space in the city, we can see that in effect the task of design is to 'fast forward' that process of evolution, so that we envisage – in the 'future perfect' tense – the way in which the fabric of the city would have evolved in response to the impulses of human habitation. These impulses are likewise constrained and influenced by that fabric in a form of unending feedback loop between inhabitants and city that echoes the relationship between wasp and orchid.

Quite how such a relationship could be modelled digitally remains an interesting challenge for urban designers. △

Kokkugia, Taipei Performing Arts Center, Taipei, China, 2008
The areas of the roof enclosing the auditoriums maintain their explicit starting geometry while the area surrounding the main circulation spine has a more complex set of requirements and reforms to negotiate these. The agents are programmed with a set of spatial imperatives while the material nature of the network creates a tendency towards equilibrium topologies that operate with a degree of structural efficiency. The network structure of the system generates both space-filling lattices and continuous surfaces where the network connections are articulated as a web of veins.

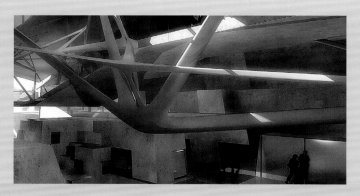

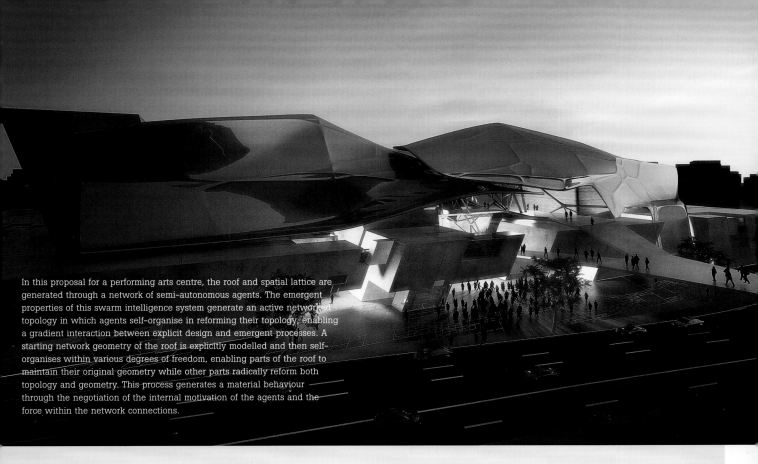

In this proposal for a performing arts centre, the roof and spatial lattice are generated through a network of semi-autonomous agents. The emergent properties of this swarm intelligence system generate an active network topology in which agents self-organise in reforming their topology, enabling a gradient interaction between explicit design and emergent processes. A starting network geometry of the roof is explicitly modelled and then self-organises within various degrees of freedom, enabling parts of the roof to maintain their original geometry while other parts radically reform both topology and geometry. This process generates a material behaviour through the negotiation of the internal motivation of the agents and the force within the network connections.

Notes

1. Steven Johnson, *Emergence: The Connected Lives of Ants, Cities and Software*, Scribner (New York), 2002. See also Mitchell Waldrop, *Complexity: The Emerging Science at the Edge of Order and Chaos*, Simon and Schuster (New York and London), 1992; John Holland, *Emergence: From Chaos to Order*, Oxford University Press (Oxford), 1998; Eric Bonabeau, Marco Dorigo and Guy Theraulaz, *Swarm Intelligence: From Natural to Artificial Systems*, Oxford University Press (New York and Oxford), 1999; Neil Leach, 'Swarm Tectonics' in N Leach, D Turnbull and C Williams (eds), *Digital Tectonics*, John Wiley & Sons (London), 2004, pp 70–77.

2. Johnson, op cit, p 104.

3. See, for example, Michael Hensel, Achim Menges and Michael Weinstock, *AD Emergence: Morphogenetic Design Strategies*, July/August 2004.

4. See Neil Leach (ed), *Rethinking Architecture: A Reader in Cultural Theory*, Routledge (London), 1997, p 147.

5. It could also be argued, for example, that certain avant-garde buildings operate collectively as a form of 'movement', even though they stand out markedly from their surroundings.

6. For a discussion of 'material computation', see Neil Leach, 'Digital Morphogenesis', *AD Theoretical Meltdown*, Jan/Feb 2009, p 35.

7. One of the limitations of fractals is that they typically involve the subdivision of an already known whole, while L-systems remain inherently hierarchical.

8. See the interview with Manuel DeLanda in this issue, pp 50–55.

9. See, for example, Patrik Schumacher, 'Parameticism: A New Global Style for Architecture and Urban Design', pp 14–23 of this issue.

10. It could be argued, however, that the surface tension in the water of a wet grid acts to self-organise the grid, and as such could be seen as a bottom-up form of material computation.

11. Kokkugia is a collaboration between Rob Stuart-Smith, Roland Snooks and Jonathan Podborsek.

12. See the Kokkugia website: www.kokkugia.com, accessed on 3 March 2009.

13. They compare this to the self-regulating system of the earth, which operates within a dynamically stable, yet fragile near-equilibrium condition that Lynn Margulis has termed 'homeorhesis'. Kevin Kelly, *Out of Control: The New Biology of Machines, Social Systems and the Economic World*, Perseus Books (New York), 1994, p 402.

14. See the Kokkugia website: www.kokkugia.com.

15. On this see Gilles Deleuze and Félix Guattari, *A Thousand Plateaus*, Athlone (London), 1988, p 32 onwards.

16. On this see Manuel DeLanda, 'Deleuze and the use of the genetic algorithm in architecture', in Neil Leach (ed), *Designing for a Digital World*, John Wiley & Sons (London), 2002, pp 117–118.

17. Deleuze and Guattari, op cit, p 432.

18. As John Holland puts it: 'Like the standing wave in front of a rock in a fast-moving stream, a city is a pattern in time.' John Holland, as quoted in Steven Johnson, op cit, p 27.

19. Deleuze and Guattari appear to be referring to the digger wasp (*Gorytes mystaceus* and *Gorytes campestris*) and fly orchid (*Ophrys insectifera*). It is curious that they do not refer to the particular sexual nature of this relationship. Usually an insect is attracted to a flower by the promise of nectar. Here, however, the sole attraction for the wasp is the potential of copulation. The orchid looks and smells like a female wasp. It attracts the male wasp, whose excited behaviour serves to dislodge pollen from the plant on to the back of the wasp, which then transfers it to another orchid as it seeks gratification elsewhere. Biologists refer to this process as one of 'pseudocopulation'. See Friedrich Barth, *Insects and Flowers*, trans MA Biederman-Thorson, George Allen and Unwin (London), 1985, pp 185–192.

20. Ansell Pearson, *Germinal Life*, Routledge (London), 1999, p 156.

21. Greg Lynn, *Folds, Bodies and Blobs*, La Lettre Volée (Brussels), 1999, p 139.

22. Deleuze and Guattari, op cit, p 10. Deleuze and Guattari's opposition to signification is an integral part of their theoretical position. Signification subscribes to the discourse of 'binary oppositions'. Moreover, it belongs to the realm of 'representation' rather than 'process', and can therefore never account for the complexity of the rhizome.

23. John Marks, *Gilles Deleuze: Vitalism and Multiplicity*, Pluto (London), 1998, p 45.

24. Deleuze and Guattari, op cit, p 11.

Morphogenetic Urbanism

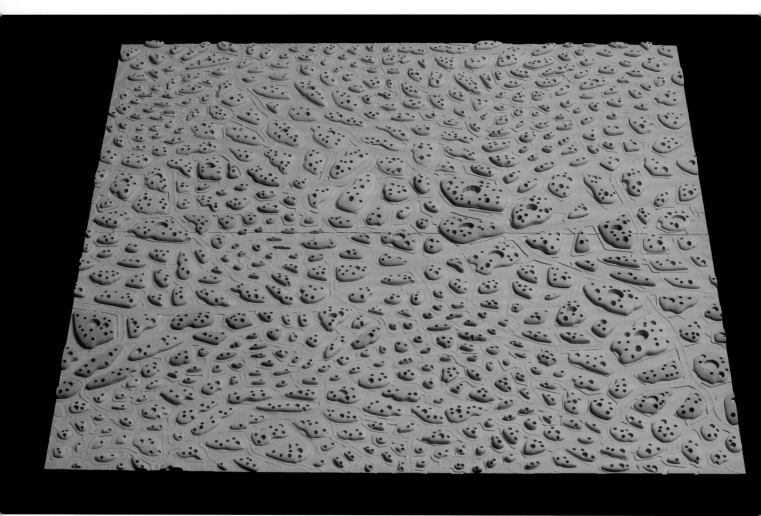

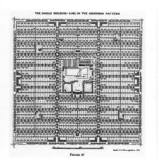

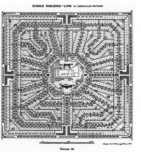

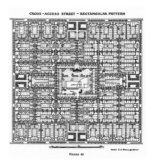

Peter Trummer pursues a morphogenetic model of urban design in which matter and form are placed in a dynamic rather than a fixed relationship. He demonstrates its application with a neighbourhood model that he has developed for the suburbs of Phoenix, Arizona, with the Second-Year Research Programme at the Berlage Institute in Rotterdam.

The hylomorphic model has dominated the relationship between matter and form within Western culture. The term 'hylomorph' indicates what is needed to design, for example, a table.[1] It derives from *hyle*, meaning wood, and *morph*, meaning form. So when we design a table by means of the hylomorphic model, we take a form (*morph*) – the image of the table we would like to design – and press it into the wood (*hyle*) – the material by which the image should come alive. The effect is a copy, a representation of what we imagined a table should look like.

However, anyone who has ever tried to hit a nail into a piece of wood knows that just as the nail can slide into the wood as smoothly as a knife into butter, the wood can be as solid and resistant as rock, twisting the metal of the nail into a snake-like form. What this means is that not only does the designer force his or her ideas into the wood, but the wood has forces that are as specific as the designer's ideas. 'They are just less active.'[2]

The hylomorphic model denies this interrelationship between ideas (form) on the one side and *hyle* (matter) on the other.[3] It assumes that form is fixed and matter is homogeneous. 'The critique of the hylomorphic schema is based on the existence between form and matter, of a zone of medium and intermediary dimension, of energetic, molecular dimensions.'[4] This zone is referred to as a 'morphogenetic space', in which both *hyle* (matter) and ideas (form) are in a dynamic relationship. It is this dynamic condition, this space of morphogenetic potential that Deleuze calls 'the machinic phylum'.[5] Let us take the example of the table. As much as wood is not just a substance in the form of a raw material but an expression of environmental forces, architects are not just agents of expression; 'from the view of social forces'[6] they are as much a raw material as wood. Thus, from the perspective of the designer, wood is the *content* of his or her idea.

'But from the perspective of the forces that went into it, it is an *expression* of sun, wind, water and carbon dioxide.'[7] The same can be said of the designer. With his or her tools, the designer 'is an agent of *expression*, but from another angle he or she is the *content* of an historically developed professional institution'.[8] This constellation of *content* and *expression* on both sides is what Deleuze proposed as a replacement of the hylomorphic model, and in recent decades the architectural world has focused on reoriginating this idea in practice and theory.[9]

In his article 'The machinic phylum',[10] Manuel DeLanda unfolds this philosophical concept and examines its significance in what he calls 'the emergence of novelty',[11] where matter is seen as an active material with 'morphogenetic capabilities' to generate different structures through the constraints of its material properties. To demonstrate what he means by this, let us instead take an example from DeLanda's article. In physics, 'a population of interacting physical entities, such as molecules, can be constrained energetically to force it to display organised collective behaviour.'[12] The example, often used to explain this behaviour, is the formation of soap bubbles. The molecules of the soap collectively minimise the tension of the surface. Each soap bubble differs according to the way the molecules organise themselves to perform the most minimal surface tension.

This dynamic condition between a *form of content* and a *form of expression* presents numerous problems for urban designers; thus, the use of computational techniques as actualisation tools is today unavoidable.[13]

So what does this mean for urbanism? The Associative Design – Urban Ecologies second-year research programme at the Berlage Institute in Rotterdam focuses on the edge of a rapidly expanding city, where the instruments of urbanisation[14] are directly applied to the raw landscape. The aim of the projects is to use the idea of a machinic phylum to generate new neighbourhood models that are able to resist homogeneity and are specific to the forces controlling their urban layouts. In terms of expression, American suburbanisation is formed by the collective desire of everyone to own their own home. But in terms of content, the forces that determine the layout of a suburb are the economic, legislative, administrative and technological regimes particular to a city.

Associative Design – Urban Ecologies, Phoenix, Arizona,
Second-Year Research Programme (Peter Trummer), Berlage Institute, Rotterdam, 2007–08
opposite top: Projected neighbourhood model. Developed from the radiation map, the model produces a population of diversified housing properties that is similar to that of Phoenix as a whole. Each of the housing envelopes is not only different in size and shape, but also incorporates various programmes and different forms of organisation. The geometry of each envelope is constrained to the least amount of radiation. Student project by Mika Watanabe and Lin Chia-Ying.
opposite bottom: Harvard design research for residential areas in the US. The diagram shows different subdivision layouts based on the same neighbourhood model. The layouts are differentiated by the various ways the individual housing units are accessed, ranging from (left to right): a) single building – line in the gridiron pattern; b) single building – line in irregular pattern; c) cul-de-sac – loop pattern; d) cross-access street – rectangular pattern; e) neighbourhood of varied dwellings – adapted to irregular topography.

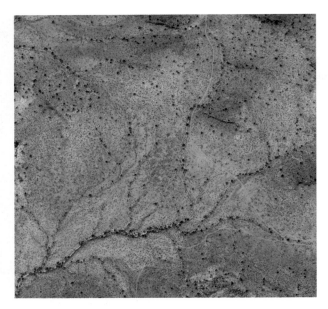

Associative Design – Urban Ecologies, Phoenix, Arizona, Second-Year Research Programme (Peter Trummer), Berlage Institute, Rotterdam, 2007–08
A quarter-mile section of the raw desert landscape of Maricopa County, Phoenix, Arizona, with its specific vegetation distribution areas, known as 'washes', which evolved out of the seasonal floods and the unconsolidated soil conditions of the Sonoran Desert basins.

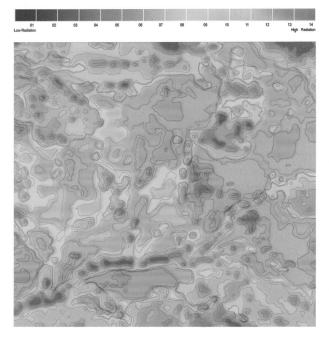

Image showing the radiation effect of the soil conditions of the desert section. The areas with a high density of vegetation show less radiation (blue) in comparison to the parts that have no vegetation at all (red). This technique is used to indicate heat island effects within the urban layout of Phoenix. Student project by Mika Watanabe and Lin Chia-Ying.

In Phoenix, Arizona, the matter to be urbanised is the Sonoran Desert. Being the world's wettest desert, it is the expression of its specific ecology, formed by the relationship between consolidated and unconsolidated rock, extreme differences in topography, seasonal floods, and the unusual flora that form its network of 'washes'.[15] However, the forces of modern planning – a culture of how to subdivide the land to produce the maximum number of similar plots – are pressed into the raw desert, erasing its distinctive ecology to create a tabula rasa. This works like the hylomorphic model described above; the idea of creating a neighbourhood is literally inserted into the material substance of the desert.

So how can we generate a morphogenetic space within which novelty can unfold during the urbanisation process. To appreciate the desert's genetic potential of form, we must understand it as active matter, not within its own ecology but in terms of the forces that try to control it. Its intensive properties must be understood, like those of surface tension which give shape to the soap bubbles referred to above, or the intense bonding energy that forms crystallised structures. Only then might the desert be able to actualise various forms of urban layouts.

The intensive properties that shape the projects presented here are the radiation of the soil and an understanding of the economic value of the Sonoran Desert. Both these territorial conditions are non-metrical properties; they can only be understood as a field in which every point is gradually differentiated from its neighbour. Each of the properties is generated by specific territorial conditions: the density of the vegetation in the case of radiation; or the manifold factors that determine economic value, such as topography, accessibility, vegetation density, water retention and noise pollution. Thus if the rules of subdivision are applied to this active matter, the specific territorial conditions would generate a differentiated field of housing units – a population[16] – that within a square mile, differ in size, internal organisation and property values to an extent that even the entire metropolitan region cannot generate.

To achieve this association between the different forms of content and expression, as a design technique for the projects an associative design protocol was developed, which unfolds across various scales – from a facade component to an environmental envelope, from single housing units to whole housing clusters – until the scale of neighbourhoods for 3,000 to 5,000 inhabitants is reached.

Associative software is mainly used to assemble several components to create an engineered master piece. Every single component relates to its own technological requirements. By changing one of its parameters, the component and all its related assemblies will be updated. The degree to which each component can change thus defines the overall appearance of the object.

Two things are radically different when associative computational techniques are used in urban planning. First, the proliferation of the same component is used to produce agglomerations; and second, the agglomerations are absorbed by regimes for which the designed component was not intended. So, for example, the proliferation of a facade element turns after a while into a structural problem, the

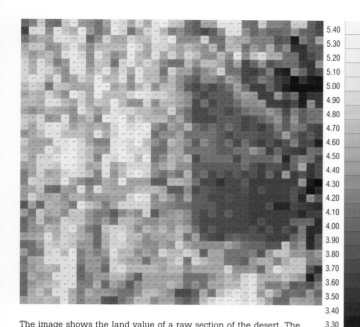

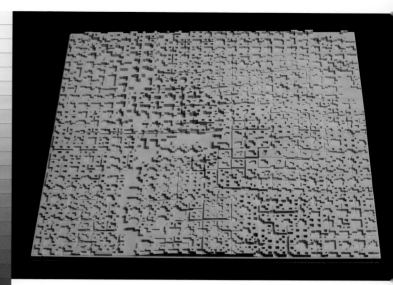

The image shows the land value of a raw section of the desert. The value is the sum of various given objectives with values ranging from 0.1 to 0.5. The objectives are: topography (TC), water retention (WR), existing feasibility (EF), vegetation density (VD), sound comport (SC), precipitation level (PL). Thus Land Value = TC+WR+EF+VD+SC+PL. Student project by Fairus Reza Razali.

LAND VALUE

5.40
5.30
5.20
5.10
5.00
4.90
4.80
4.70
4.60
4.50
4.40
4.30
4.20
4.10
4.00
3.90
3.80
3.70
3.60
3.50
3.40
3.30
3.20
3.10
3.00

Projected neighbourhood model. Produced from the economic properties of the desert, the model actualises a population of housing units ranging from US$50.000 to US$1 million. The diversity is based on four different market factors: a) front footage; b) size; c) amount of housing unit per plot; d) square footage of the living area. Student project by Fairus Reza Razali.

accumulation of the housing units turns into a problem of accessibility and might have an effect on the land value, and the housing clusters define beyond a certain scale, the social strata of the neighbourhood.

Thus it can be concluded that in order to construct a morphogenetic approach to urbanism, the use of associative design techniques needs to be evaluated in terms of their assembly. It is less the intelligence of the geometrical model that unfolds morphogenetic potential; rather, as in matter, it is the collective behaviour of the geometrical components, whether facade elements or housing unit that determines how they perform through their agglomerations. ∆

Notes

1. The example is taken from Brian Massumi, *A User's Guide to Capitalism and Schizophrenia*, MIT Press (Cambridge, MA and London), 1992, pp 12–13.
2. Ibid.
3. Gilles Deleuze and Félix Guattari, *A Thousand Plateaus: Capitalism and Schizophrenia*, Continuum (New York) and The Athlone Press (London), 1987, p 408–9.
4. Ibid.
5. Ibid.
6. Massumi, op cit, pp 12–13.
7. Ibid.
8. Ibid.
9. See, for example, Michael Hensel, Achim Menges and Michael Weinstock, *AD Emergence: Morphogenetic Design Strategies*, July/August 2004, and Neil Leach, 'Digital Morphogenesis', in Luigi Prestinenza Puglisi, *AD Theoretical Meltdown*, Jan/Feb 2009, pp 32–7.
10. Manuel DeLanda, 'The machinic phylum', in, *TechnoMorphica*, V2_Publisher (Amsterdam), 1997. Taken from the V2-Archive: http://framework.v2.nl/archive/archive/node/text/.xslt/nodenr-70071.
11. For a discussion of the idea of 'emergence', see Neil Leach, 'Swarm Urbanism', pp 56–63 of this issue.
12. DeLanda, op cit.
13. 'Problems' refers less to thinking about them in terms of solution, but rather to Todd May's description of problems as open fields of discussion. See Todd May, *Gilles Deleuze: An Introduction*, Cambridge University Press (New York), 2005, p 83.
14. 'Urbanisation' refers to the original definition given by the progressive Spanish urban planner Ildefonso Cerdà in his 1867 *General Theory of Urbanization*, whereby he describes the five bases of urbanism: the technical, the economic, the legislative, the administrative and the political.
15. For the entire research projects, see the second-year research programme by Peter Trummer (participants: Tsung-Jen Chang, Botsung Chiu, Hsu Tzu-En, Dae-Won Kwak, Kyo Suk Lee, Lin Chia-Ying, Fairuz Reza Razali and Mika Watanabe), Research Report Nr 14, *Associative Design – Urban Ecologies, Phoenix Arizona*, Berlage Institute (Rotterdam), 2007/2008.
16. For a further discussion of the idea of population, see Peter Trummer, 'Population Thinking in the Age of Bio-Politics', *Archis*, Vol 18, 2009, pp 68–71.

Text © 2009 John Wiley & Sons Ltd. Images: pp 64(t), 66(b) © Berlage Institute Rotterdam/Mika Watanabi/Lin Chia-Ying; p 64(b), From Thomas Adams, *Metropolitan America: The Design of Residential Areas, Basic Considerations, Principles, and Methods*, Arno Press (New York), 1974. Reprint of the edition published by Harvard University Press, Cambridge, issued as V 6 of Harvard City Planning Studies; p 66(t) © Berlage Institute Rotterdam/Peter Tijhuis; p 67 © Berlage Institute Rotterdam/Fairus Reza Razali

Digital
Towers

Code, it would seem, is everywhere. We are beginning to understand that much of our natural environment is based on rule-based behaviours, from the emergent swarm intelligence of flocks of birds and schools of fish, to the complex patterns of snowflakes, ferns, seashells and zebra skins. And nothing escapes. Not even the human body. The human genome is being mapped out and sequenced by scientists to provide a genetic blueprint of human life itself. In this context, it is hardly surprising that architects are now beginning to explore similar principles in the design studio. The apparent primacy of these codes opens up the possibility of modelling systems through digital means, and with it the potential of using digital technologies to breed structures. An ever-growing group of young architects is using the technique of 'scripting' — the manipulation of digital code — to produce radically innovative architectural environments. A new generation of structures is being created that recognises the potential of the computer not just as a sophisticated drafting and rendering tool, but also as a potentially powerful tool in the generation of designs themselves. This selection of digital towers offers a glimpse of the forms that can be generated either by the use of code itself, or by the use of parametric modelling softwares. Five student projects have been selected, alongside five projects by architectural practitioners. None of the towers has been built. But it is not as if these towers are merely utopian follies. On the contrary, the techniques that they illustrate are precisely those that are informing advanced architectural production today. We are witnessing a shift in the status of digital operations from a marginalised domain of experimentation to a central role in the production of architectural information. Few significant architectural offices can afford not to engage with advanced digital modelling, which was once limited to the province of the avant-garde. Indeed, many are developing their own in-house digital research units. So, too, we are witnessing the creation of a fresh and highly innovative vocabulary of architectural forms, generated by the algorithmic potential of the computer — from the proliferating logic of cellular aggregation, to the adaptive, parametric behaviour of distributive systems mutating across a field condition.

Neil Leach

Testa & Weiser, Automorphic
Strand Tower, 2006.

PeristalCity

Neri Oxman and Mitchel Joachim, MIT Computation Group (William Mitchell), Massachusetts Institute of Technology (MIT), Cambridge, Massachusetts, 2006

If there is one building that characterises the Modernist project of the 20th century and represents its aspirations it is the skyscraper. The Peristal Tower project attempts to reconsider and critically revisit this well-celebrated typology in the context of the ever-growing city of the 21st century. It aims to develop the notion of vertical mobility as an approach to the changing needs of both the individual and the collective. As the sole signifier of vertical rigidity, both programmatic and performative, elevator and core have been dematerialised through the invention of PeristalCity. Intended to dematerialise the organisational distribution of spaces that are influenced predominantly by the typology, PeristalCity seeks to rethink the structural and material logic of vertically distributed environments. It does so by introducing a new concept which breaks away from the dichotomy between space and circulation. This new concept of space is motivated by research into a new technology which seeks to overcome traditional typological spatial and structural constructs: an inhabitable pocket (living and working unit) contained within a flexible element. It is a module that flows in a vertical communicative field with its surrounding members. Its position is determined and managed by a responsive signalling system controlled by structural, environmental and spatial stimuli.

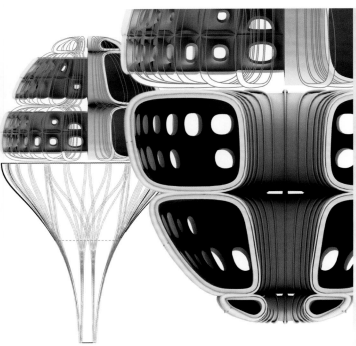

SWELLS: A PROTOTYPE FOR DENSE HIGH-RISE CITYSCAPES

Biothing (Alisa Andrasek), 2004

This project is conceived out of a desire to address the accelerated condition of design and construction in China. It works as a simulation tool for architects to test various structural and organisational patterns that can then be instantiated in the context of particular designs, and addresses the historically rigid high-rise typology. Through thickening and thinning, the Swells reinforce and expand the structural envelope of a tall building, and forces are transmitted across its poly-directional structural network by a system of horizontal connective hinges. Swells are generated through an ascending population of cellular agents whose collective transformation frequencies are indexed by the swelling intensities of the emergent global structure. Cellular layers come in and out of phase, thickening and thinning the skin tissue. The Swells form parametrically modulated symptoms of an affected skin, driven by the multiple vectors moving away from the core plane. Scalar modulation of spatial fabric can be retextured to allow for maximum openness or divisibility of space. Statistical propagation of programming molecules offers opportunities for populating high-rise territories more compatible with the flexible nature of current cultures of inhabitation. The recurrent organisation patterns that emerge form diverse neighbourhood relationships that allow for endless programmatic affinities.

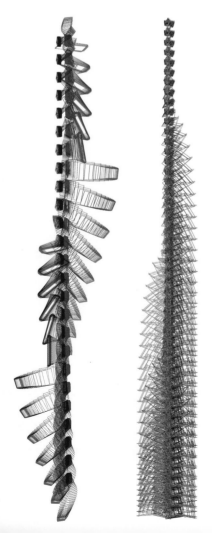

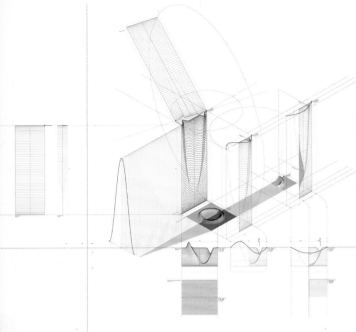

RISING MASSES

Max Kahlen, Diploma Unit 5 (George Legendre),
Architectural Association, London, 2008

The Rising Masses project addresses verticality and the madness
of repetition. It features a residential high-rise building, floating
within the regimented grid of Singapore's office district. Writing
form mathematically defines the basic concept, using the notation
of functions and equations to confront both the abstract
development of a syntax of form and the concept of 'automatic
writing', where form is driven purely by industrial performance
ratios such as floor-area ratios, maximum building heights,
facade-to-area ratios and so on. The scheme proposes two 6-
metre (19.7-foot) thick building slabs, each 180 metres (590.5
feet) high and 40 metres (131.2 feet) long. This building typology
generates spaces within the slabs that constantly face each other,
and thereby creates an awareness of the extremely thin
proportions of the building that serve to emphasise a lifestyle
characterised by constant confrontation with the extremely dense
surrounding urban fabric. On their external facades the slabs
reflect the monotony of the neighbouring buildings, while on their
interior facades this monotony dissolves as they deform into
vertical folds. The folds stabilise and connect each slab and provide
external vertical circulation. The transformation from the rigid
curtain-wall facade into an external structural grid blurs the spatial
boundary of inside and outside, and interlocks the interstitial
space between the two slabs with the dense urban environment.

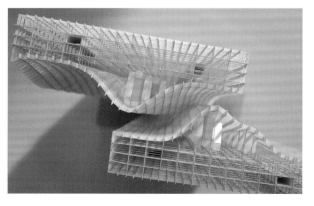

EVOLUTIONARY COMPUTATION

moh architects (Jens Mehlan, Christoph Opperer and Jorg Hugo), 2006

The claim that form follows function seems to be most valid when looking at biological systems. In order to survive, biological structures evolve as highly complex systems whose aim is to provide an optimal solution for any given requirement. Every organism and life form emerges through a process of evolutionary self-organisation. While the principles of morphogenesis tend to become an increasingly attractive paradigm in the field of architectural design, and while the aesthetic appeal of natural forms has always been important to architects and designers, the inherent principles of these systems have gained significance ever since evolutionary and genetic computation have been used for design and optimisation purposes. The Evolutionary Computation project investigates the potential of evolutionary and genetic computation in a more holistic approach to architectural and structural design. It takes advantage of evolutionary form-finding strategies through the use of material self-organisation under load and gravity. Instead of post-optimising the structure in the final stage of the process, the project embraces these methods and deliberately deploys them as the very tools of the design at the outset. Evolutionary and genetic computation strategies are here used for finding an optimised form (based on given demands) to create a differentiated and complex architecture.

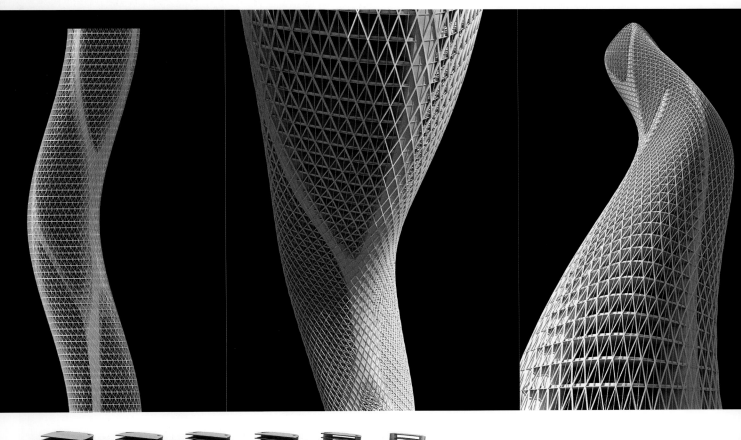

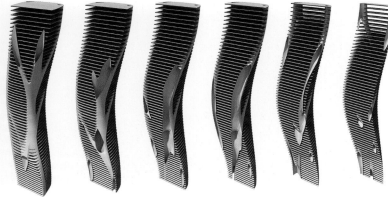

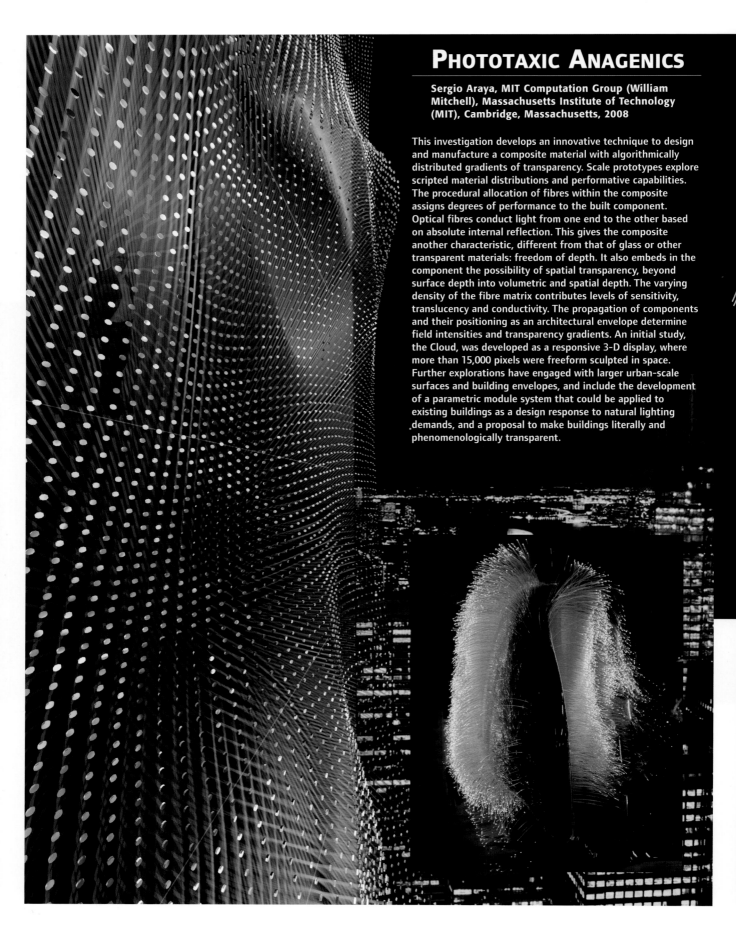

PHOTOTAXIC ANAGENICS

Sergio Araya, MIT Computation Group (William Mitchell), Massachusetts Institute of Technology (MIT), Cambridge, Massachusetts, 2008

This investigation develops an innovative technique to design and manufacture a composite material with algorithmically distributed gradients of transparency. Scale prototypes explore scripted material distributions and performative capabilities. The procedural allocation of fibres within the composite assigns degrees of performance to the built component. Optical fibres conduct light from one end to the other based on absolute internal reflection. This gives the composite another characteristic, different from that of glass or other transparent materials: freedom of depth. It also embeds in the component the possibility of spatial transparency, beyond surface depth into volumetric and spatial depth. The varying density of the fibre matrix contributes levels of sensitivity, translucency and conductivity. The propagation of components and their positioning as an architectural envelope determine field intensities and transparency gradients. An initial study, the Cloud, was developed as a responsive 3-D display, where more than 15,000 pixels were freeform sculpted in space. Further explorations have engaged with larger urban-scale surfaces and building envelopes, and include the development of a parametric module system that could be applied to existing buildings as a design response to natural lighting demands, and a proposal to make buildings literally and phenomenologically transparent.

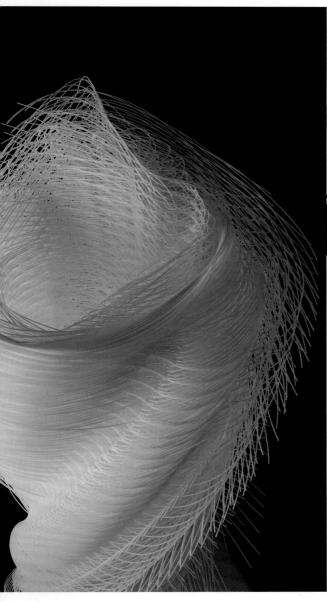

AUTOMORPHIC STRAND TOWER

Testa & Weiser (Peter Testa, Devyn Weiser and Emily White), 2006

The Automorphic Strand Tower introduces an environmentally sensitive 21st-century construction system based on the self-organising properties of extreme fibre networks. It draws on many sources ranging from tissue engineering and textile technology to organic templating. The tower instantiates agency at the level of individual fibres and fibre groups that organise recursively to create extreme networks of unprecedented complexity. This emergent strand morphology was generated using software developed by Testa & Weiser, and coded through an iterative templating and scripting process. The underlying principle of fibre agency and affiliation demonstrates the potential of coding structures for anexact construction. The ultra-light nested fibre structure builds strength and resilience through a massive redundancy of elements that challenges conventional models of structural and environmental performance. The tower is built on site using an innovative automorphic construction technique developed specifically for the project, whereby robotically spun basalt fibre groups form nested structural and spatial layers. In effect the project consists of fibre strands that are robotically spun into place like candy floss. In this way the tower manifests in real time the concurrent development of material properties, spatial patterns, design technology and fabrication techniques.

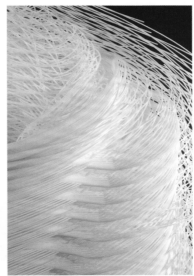

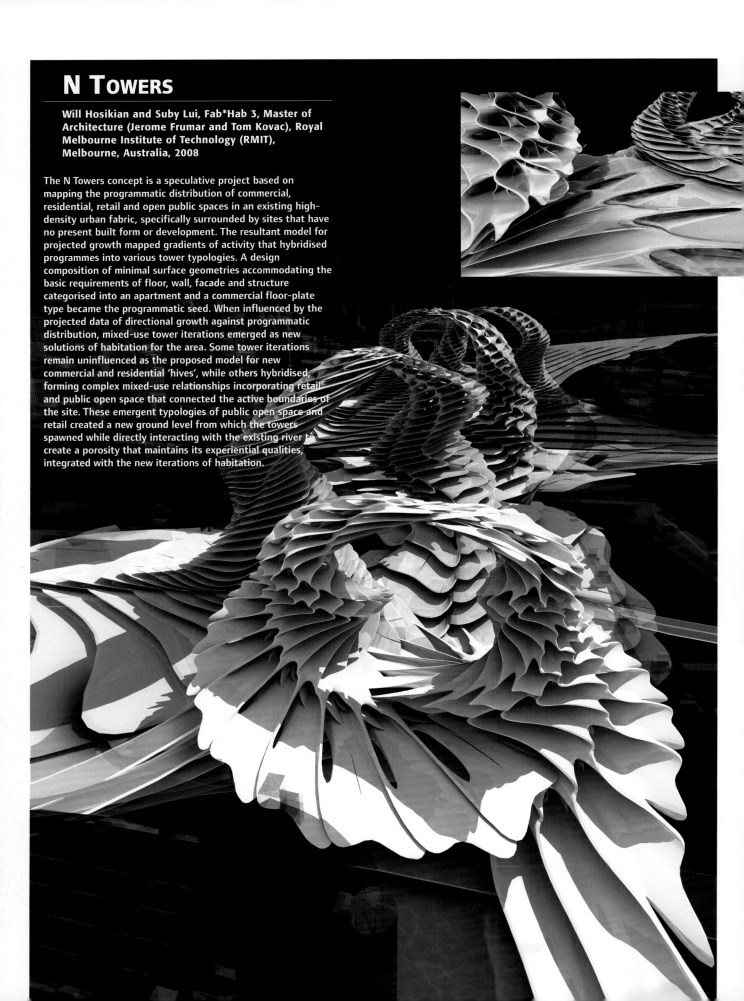

N Towers

Will Hosikian and Suby Lui, Fab*Hab 3, Master of Architecture (Jerome Frumar and Tom Kovac), Royal Melbourne Institute of Technology (RMIT), Melbourne, Australia, 2008

The N Towers concept is a speculative project based on mapping the programmatic distribution of commercial, residential, retail and open public spaces in an existing high-density urban fabric, specifically surrounded by sites that have no present built form or development. The resultant model for projected growth mapped gradients of activity that hybridised programmes into various tower typologies. A design composition of minimal surface geometries accommodating the basic requirements of floor, wall, facade and structure categorised into an apartment and a commercial floor-plate type became the programmatic seed. When influenced by the projected data of directional growth against programmatic distribution, mixed-use tower iterations emerged as new solutions of habitation for the area. Some tower iterations remain uninfluenced as the proposed model for new commercial and residential 'hives', while others hybridised, forming complex mixed-use relationships incorporating retail and public open space that connected the active boundaries of the site. These emergent typologies of public open space and retail created a new ground level from which the towers spawned while directly interacting with the existing river to create a porosity that maintains its experiential qualities, integrated with the new iterations of habitation.

FIBROUS TOWER

Kokkugia (Roland Snooks, Rob Stuart-Smith, Juan De Marco and Timo Carl), 2008

This fibrous concrete shell tower for Hong Kong emerged from a series of earlier studies, undertaken with Rojkind Arquitectos, of exoskeleton tower typologies. The project compresses the structural and tectonic hierarchies of contemporary tower design into a single shell whose articulation self-organises in response to multiple design criteria, incorporating structural, spatial, environmental and ornamental imperatives. The initial topology of the shell's articulation is algorithmically generated through a cell division procedure in response to the tower geometry. The shell is both performative and ornamental, and operates as a non-linear structure where load is distributed through a network of paths, relying on collectively organised intensities rather than on a hierarchy of discrete elements. The load-bearing shell and slender floor plates enable the building to remain column-free. Although the external articulation is geometrically complex, it operates within the thickness of comparatively simple shell geometry, enabling the use of conventional formwork techniques to construct a highly differentiated tower. The localised spatial complexity and intensifications in the shell geometry suggest a rereading of the shell as epidermis – a performative outer skin that integrates a set of discrete concerns through the cellular structure of a continuous surface.

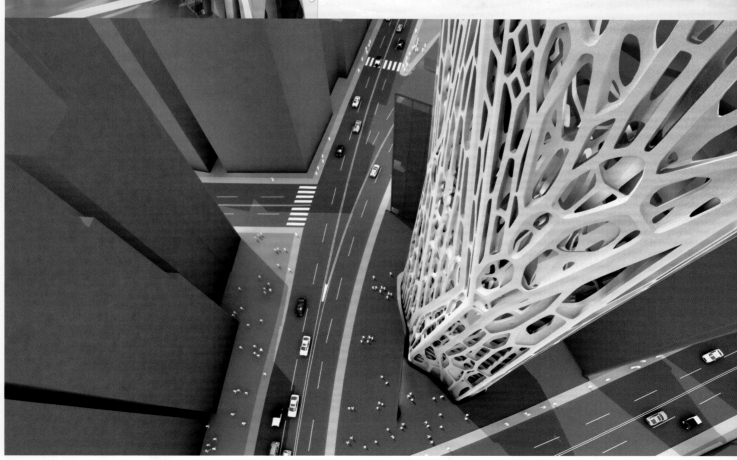

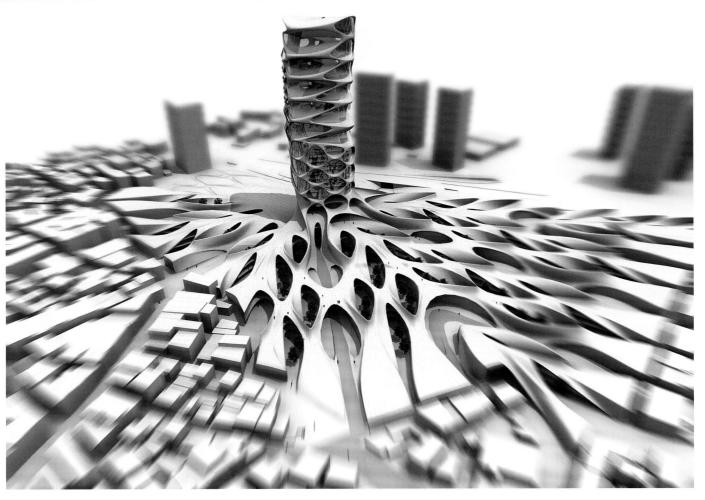

COMPRESSED COMPLEXITY

Peter Mitterer and Matthias Moroder, Studio Hadid
(Zaha Hadid and Patrik Schumacher), University of
Applied Arts, Vienna, Austria, 2006

Compressed Complexity rethinks the typology of the classical
skyscraper by combining a largely horizontal public shopping base
and a mono-functional stacked private office or housing slab. This
has implications for circulation, public accessibility, transition
between programmes and the formal distinction between base
and slab. Addressing this issue, the typical horizontal system of
public programmes is superimposed on to a vertical organisational
pattern and subsequently developed as a diagonal spatial
prototype. Adaptations of this basic prototype are generated to
produce various functional formulations. The diagonal allocation
of the public programme enables a continuous vertical public
space that enhances the mix of functions and facilitates
navigation around the site. The residential landscape forms a
dense horizontal urban fabric that responds to the scale of the
site and allows it to blend into the existing context. As the
surface folds up from the landscape into the tower, the geometric
features are mutated and do not repeat. Different rhythms are
achieved by two rates of change adjacent to one another, driven
by internal organisational issues, and hybridised to produce a
range of formal features in the tower.

RESONANCE: BETWEEN REPETITION AND DIFFERENCE

THEVERYMANY (Marc Fornes, Vincent Nowak and Claudia Corcilius), 2006

'Any tower is multiple': such an assumption can easily be made by looking at towers as stacked objects. Once efficiency and other economic criteria have been introduced, such stacking usually becomes periodic – with the floor constituting the common period. Increasing the resolution through subdivision into smaller parts (such as rooms or desks) introduces modulation and higher frequencies. Resonance: Between Repetition and Difference is a design research exercise investigating such relations/rhythms through explicit and encoded protocols: 'explicit' because they are the result of precise and ordered sets of procedures, and 'encoded' because they are written within a scripted computational language (in this case Rhinoscript). The design constraints have been encapsulated within multiple logistical functions called 'modulo' operations in relation to floors, rooms or parts, each informed either through global parameters (such as overall twisting acceleration) or by the previous step. One step follows on from another in an unbroken chain of cause and effect which is completely predictable. In principle, the resultant morphology should therefore be completely orderly and deterministic. But in practice, due to the high number of periods in a tower, even small periodic increments can produce large amplitudinal vibrations that constantly repeat their instructional sequences and generate tiny variations. ∆

Texts and images compiled by Neil Leach

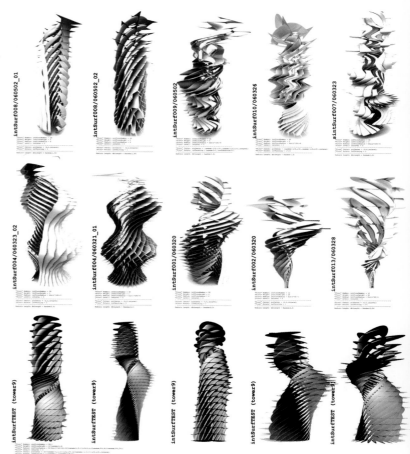

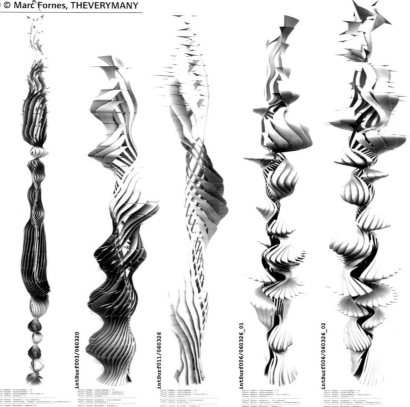

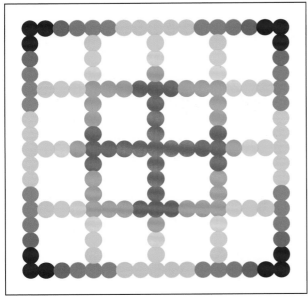
1a

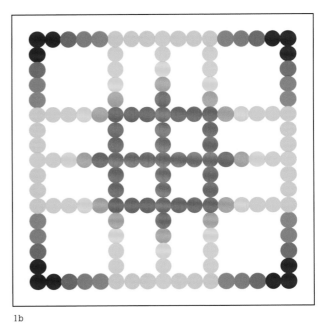
1b

Spatial Design Economies

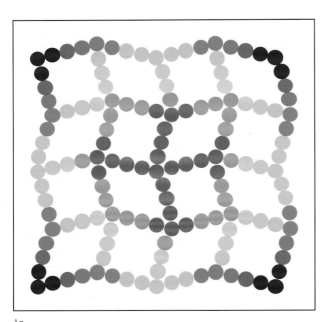
1c

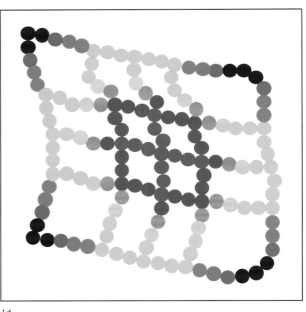
1d

The digital revolution has enabled an influx of data that has allowed us to analyse cities in ways that could never previously be anticipated. How, though, might this data be constructively applied in a manner that could shape and improve not only urban patterns, but also people's economic and social prospects? **Alain Chiaradia** looks at how space syntax spatial analyses might enable spatial design economies in the future, with special reference to London and the Borough of Tower Hamlets in particular.

2a

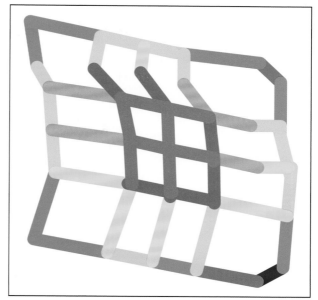
2b

Today more than ever sociocultural and economic development means urbanised development: city regions are recognised as the locus of a nation's wealth. An understanding of spatial settings has been brought centre stage in economics thanks in large measure to the work of Paul Krugman, awarded the 2008 Nobel Prize in the discipline. Krugman's achievement has been to integrate the previously disparate fields of economic geography and trade. He masterfully addresses one of spatial economics' profound challenges, introducing a true spatial dimension. In spatial economics, spatial settings tend to be either fairly simplistic (a line, a circle, a set of crossroads, of discs; nested hexagons; homogeneous continuous space, city regions) or overly complex, as in spatial econometrics, and so of limited use to the spatial designer.

What precisely does the digital city herald? On the empirical front it augers the advent of a mass of real-time information on cities, data that are both increasingly diversified and spatially defined. The data reinforce the discomforting picture of divergence not only between urban regions but at much smaller intra-urban local area level. For example, west and east Inner London rank first

and third in terms of output growth since 1997, with Milton Keynes taking second place. Inner London's position at the top of the regional table is now threatened by the recession and job losses in the City. Nevertheless, the differential in wealth within Inner East London is enormous and persistent. Recent experience of urban renaissance in UK core-city regions indicates that it was possible to close the gap at city region level at least partially. In spatial economics it is this phenomenon that constitutes the essence of the convergence debate: the expectation that urban areas will develop at different rates until they all enjoy pretty much the same standard of wealth. The poorest grow at the fastest rate. To paraphrase Rem Koolhaas, this is the unclear tale of Lagos, a city that will outpace London or, alternatively, of a London that in the near future will become more like Lagos. Yet everything we observe points to the opposite, to a lack of convergence. Herein lies the continuing challenge of understanding and designing out, if at all possible, those disparities between and within cities that remain stubbornly entrenched. Human capital, social networks as powerful forces, have been propounded as explanations. People migrate to capital, and not the other way around, albeit there are exceptions. How does human and urban capital co-locate? Does spatial design matter? How to evaluate spatial design?

Figure 1: Measuring design effect – relative metric distance
opposite: Simple spatial models of notional urban street layout are used that have the same area coverage, street length, number of places and same connectivity. The spatial layout is changed by urban block design variations (see Figures 1a and 1b). For each place (dot) the distance to all other places is calculated and aggregated to arrive at a relative distance measure for each place. Ranking relative distance, magenta indicates the nearest places to everywhere (centrality level), to dark blue, the furthest away to everywhere (dispersion level). The summing up of all relative distance is then an indicator of overall spatial dispersion (increase) or agglomeration (decrease).

Figure 2: Measuring design effect – relative geometric distance
top: The figures here show how the transformed street layout (2a and 2b) has been encoded in space syntax as a minimum line-set mapped according to changes in geometry. The relative distance indicators use the same principle as previously but apply a geometric distance unit. The relative geometric distance between two places, A and Z, is the shortest geometric path, the sum of angles between successive parts of the path as we move along the shortest geometric route between A and Z. The geometric distance along a straight line is zero. The spatial layout geometric variations, their design, are now captured and differentiated.

What is best known about space syntax is its revealing of the relationship between spatial layout and people walking – walking is the degree zero of transport. Without transport spatial design is immaterial.

Space Syntax Measures of Spatial Design Effects

Space syntax was originally conceived by Professor Bill Hillier and his colleagues at the Bartlett, UCL in the 1980s as a software tool to help the spatial designer simulate some of the likely design effects of concurrent spatial geometries on perceived and revealed spatial legibility and distance. Subsequently, space syntax has grown to become a tool-set used around the world in a variety of research domains and design applications. It has been extensively applied in the fields of interior architecture, large public architecture and urban design. Over the past decade, space syntax techniques have also been used for research in fields as diverse as archaeology, information technology, urban and human geography, and anthropology.

What is best known about space syntax is its revealing of the relationship between spatial layout and people walking – walking is the degree zero of transport. Without transport spatial design is immaterial. Recently this connection has been shown to hold true for multiscale motorised transports and socioeconomic activity locations, findings that have important socioeconomic ramifications.

Space syntax is a set of relative distance metrics embedded in software tools for the analysis of spatial design configurations – the physical arrangement and organisation of spaces. This is spatial design of all kinds of spaces from a room, house, building, neighbourhood or city to a megacity region. To understand why this is positive design description, it is necessary to grasp the particular peculiarities of space syntax indicators.

What is relative distance? Consider adding some new place to the existing street layout. In an absolute distance system, the Euclidian system, this would entail the seemingly far-fetched idea that adding a stretch of street anywhere in the UK would change all the distances in the UK. In space syntax it actually has this effect, and on reflection one could argue that this is intuitively accurate.

The distance covered by a person, animal, vehicle or object along a straight, curved or sinuous path from point A to point Z is what separates A from Z. Let's imagine that we want to capture what happens to distance as we move along between A and Z, a distance system centred on the moving person, animal, vehicle or object. As we move away from A our distance from A is increasing while our distance from Z is decreasing. While moving, these distance variations also hold true between us and any other location that might be of interest. Space syntax relative distance assessment captures this spatial agglomeration and reachability effect, one that is primarily influenced by geographic location and layout design, and calls this measure 'integration'.

The 'choice' measure is the number of shortest paths between all other places that pass through a given place; in other words, the level of path overlap or amount of flow in a given place from all other places. This can be interpreted as the place of potential high co-presence or crowding/congestion depending on capacity and mode of transport (other assessment measures are also used, such as geometric continuity and connectivity).

The specification of relative distance from one place to everywhere else can be varied to accommodate a range of distance-time budgets, such as 400-metre/5-minute walk, 800-metre/10-minute walk, 2-kilometre (1.2-mile) cycling, riding public transport or 10-kilometre (6.2-mile) driving. This specification is called the radius. It implies that for each place the relative distance indicators will only be measured to every other place within the chosen radius. For example, in the UK the majority of car-based trips are less than 3 kilometres (1.9 miles), thus we may want an understanding of spatial layout effect at that particular radius of 2 to 5 kilometres (1.2 to 3.2 miles).

Figures 1a and 1b illustrate something quite remarkable in terms of spatial economics: the same input produces a 2 per cent change in output. This shows that design is a total factor of productivity (TFP) – design accounts for effects in total output not caused by inputs, and TFP can be directly measured. In economics the weather, a factor largely outside our control, is considered a TFP. More amenable to design and TFP change is technology growth and efficiency. In design terms 1c and 1d show that relative metric distance does not account for major design effects, in other words geometric changes are not captured. Figures 2a and 2b explain a space syntax alternative.

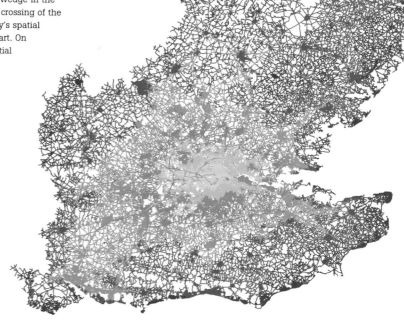

Figure 3: Greater Southeast of England spatial agglomeration: radius 50 kilometres
One of the benefits of urbanisation is agglomeration. Spatial agglomeration can be evaluated at different scales by calculating integration according to different radii. The spaces coloured red are the ones that benefit most from spatial agglomeration. To the west the M25 orbital, the radial M40 and M4 motorways, and in between a supergrid with access to Heathrow airport, are all coloured red. This is the successful western wedge in the London plan. To the east the M25 and the Dartford crossing of the Thames are coloured less red. The Thames Gateway's spatial agglomeration is no match for its western counterpart. On the east side the Lea Valley is a major break in spatial agglomeration on the east–west axis as is the Thames on the north–south axis.

Figures 3 and 4 show an integration map (spatial agglomeration and reachability) of the Greater Southeast of England (radius 50 kilometres/31 miles), and choice map (flow amount concentration) of Inner East London (radius 5 kilometres/3.1 miles). Spatial agglomeration, reachability, flow amount and congestion are here analysed at the multiscale (400 metres/1,312 feet, 800 metres/2,625 feet, 1,200 metres/3,937 feet, 2 kilometres/1.24 miles, 5 kilometres/3.1 miles, 10 kilometres/6.2 miles and beyond).

These spatial formalisations are empirically linked to multiscale transport systems and a range of urban socioeconomic consequences in different urban cultures worldwide. For example, choice has a high level of correlation at low radius with pedestrian activity, and a higher radius with cycling and driving route preferences and public transport access points as well as systematic linkages with the sites of socioeconomic activities.

Aggregating multiradius spatial layout analyses shows that urban core functions (non-residential, about 20 per cent overall) have particular spatial location signatures that combine highest choice values at high, medium and low range radius. The fundamental concepts that explain these relationships are of two types: cognitive and dynamic.

Human spatial cognition and memory capacity are limited; city layout geometry is not as complex as that of a maze (where people normally lose their way) and can be as geometrically simple as in a gridiron, which is easy to navigate if differentiated by architecture. The space syntax geometric measure captures these degrees of the layout's geometric design complexity/simplicity.

Using a motorised vehicle to speed movement requires a particular layout geometry – a maze is not an easy place to rush through; equally, a gridiron with all its junctions is an impediment to speed. Space syntax geometric complexity/simplicity, connectivity measures and metric radius index geometry can be used to interface the speeds of various transport modes.

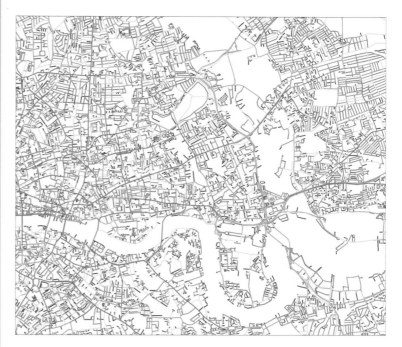

Figure 4: East London and the Olympic site, spatial congestion: radius 5 kilometres
The disadvantage of spatial agglomeration is congestion. One factor that causes congestion is the lack of spatial connectivity that concentrates all the traffic into a few routes. The spaces coloured red are those that have the highest level of path overlap in relation to spatial agglomeration within a 5-kilometre (3.1-mile) radius. To the northeast is the site of the 2012 Olympic Park. The Lea Valley creates a noticeable radial break between East London and the dense web of the City of London. The challenge for spatial design is to maximise spatial agglomeration and maintain or decrease spatial congestion. The Olympic legacy spatial framework aims to achieve this objective by providing new east–west linkages.

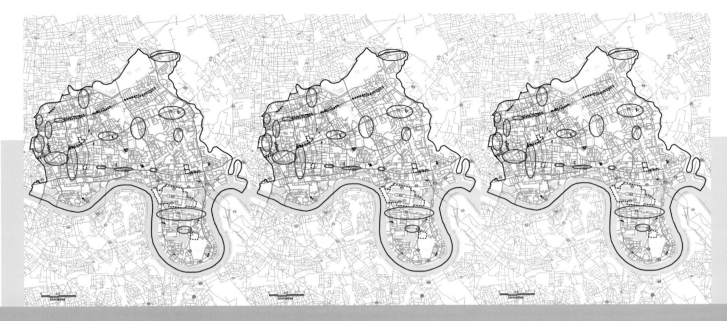

Figure 5: Multiscale spatial design analyses
In the London Borough of Tower Hamlets (LBTH), 70 to 80 per cent of non-residential urban functions – destination clusters that characterise centres and public transport access points – are located on only 20 per cent of the spatial network. The LBTH centre locations are indicated by dotted black lines. This 20 per cent has specific multiscale spatial signatures revealed by space syntax analyses: using the relative geometric distance and choice, the 20 per cent highest level of path overlap is shown (from left to right) for 10-kilometre (6.2-mile), 2-kilometre (1.2-mile) and 800-metre (half-mile) radii. Emerging centres are registered in blue.

Inner London:
Tower Hamlets Town Centre Spatial Strategy to 2025

Just as a nation's wealth is predominantly located and generated in its city regions, so urban centres are the locations and generators of a city region's wealth. Understanding how these centres' spatial configurations operate in relation to their local markets and beyond is a challenge. Unfortunately, spatial and urban economics has little to say about intra-urban macro, meso or micro spatial scale. In this context, London is of particular interest as a centre of population that achieved the largest city size in global terms (8.5 million inhabitants in 1939) before the advent of mass car use (one car for every 10 households in 1939). London has a polycentric network of hubs: two internationally designated centres (Knightsbridge and the West End), 10 metropolitan centres (mainly in Outer London), 30 major centres, some 150 district centres and more than 1,300 neighbourhood centres. Let us take as an example the London Borough of Tower Hamlets (LBTH). Over the past 60 years the spatial form in Tower Hamlets in East London, has been significantly altered. In the light of these changes, LBTH has commissioned a consortium comprising Space Syntax Ltd, not-for-profit regeneration consultancy Renaisi and planning consultants Roger Tym & Partners to develop a town centre spatial strategy which will allow the borough to meet its aspirations, which are focused on competitiveness and cohesion. In the last 100 years

LBTH has undergone radical socioeconomic and physical transformation. A harbour developed during the heyday of the British Empire was heavily bombed during the Second World War and postwar carpet planning radically altered it in terms of both architecture and infrastructure. In recent years, the City of London establishment has expanded eastwards and a new financial centre, Canary Wharf, has emerged in its midst. Tower Hamlets is a borough of stark contrasts and wide social and economic disparities. To meet the borough's spatial design needs, an understanding of social and spatial sorting in relation to centre spatial ecology is the challenge that the digital city will help to address.

Sharing, Matching and Learning: The Dynamic of Agglomeration Economies

From agglomeration emerge centres that facilitate the sharing of many indivisible public goods, production facilities and markets. For example, indivisible public goods range from museums, opera houses, sport facilities and schools, to airports, train stations and even power plants. In their turn, such centres facilitate matching; centres have never operated solely as shopping high streets, and a wider range of uses, such as leisure, services and civic functions co-locate. People like to live near shops, and shops need to be near their customers, but 'near' is relative and, while this might explain the shopping centre, it does not cover every aspect of a centre. Centres command more or less of their local market and even act as loci of import/export: they attract customers from elsewhere, from the not so near to the very far. London's success has acted as a magnet, drawing the most wealthy to live in its most desirable areas, rather than in the UK counties' hinterland. LBTH is no exception. The contribution of London to the UK's total economy increases considerably when measured by where

Figure 6: Centre spatial form

Contiguous and pervasive centres: These centres have blurred edges and are pervasive and contiguous in the main centre. In London this configuration can be found on the central activity zone and its fringe. The pervasive configuration allows for a varied relationship between quality of experience, the local market and multiscale transport.

Offline, online centres: located just off main arterials, but still on linear streets, this centre configuration, if well embedded in the local market, provides both multiscale transport interface and a better-quality experience.

Online centres: located on main arterials such as the strategic road network. They have locational advantage in terms of their multiscale transport accessibility and their embedding in the local market. Conflict due to the co-existence of high- and low-speed modes of transport greatly affects the quality of experience. This is the most typical centre in London: the high street.

Offline pod centres: pushing the previous configuration to the extreme, this spatial configuration is represented by shopping malls or big box retail parks. Such a configuration sometimes offers excellent public transport provision and total design experience, yet lacks local market embedding.

people live rather than by where they work. Interestingly, centre local market potential expenditure comes in surprising guises: gentrified areas with low population density and high-income inhabitants are equal in value size to populous areas of high density and low income. The former exhibit volatile spending patterns and a taste for spatial diversity allowed by high spatial mobility and low impact on incomes; the latter market is much more localised yet its taste for diversity is not absent.

As the number of agents trying to match increases, so the expected quality and chance of each match improves, whether in terms of people, things or ideas. By bringing together large numbers of people, centres may thus facilitate learning. Put differently, the learning opportunities offered by cities could provide a strong justification for their existence. Moreover, the advantages cities offer for learning are manifest not only because they are the main sites for cutting-edge technologies, but also because they are optimal places for the acquisition of skills and 'everyday' incremental knowledge creation, diffusion and accumulation (knowing how, knowing who, knowing what). The bringing together is mostly a layout design effect. Sharing, matching and learning all involve transport at different scale/speeds and pausing. Without transport space is immaterial; sharing, matching and learning are difficult without pausing. As seen in the notional spatial models, spatial layout design gives some places a differential spatial advantage: a certain level of centrality profile at different radii. Figure 5 shows how

space syntax spatial layout design analyses of non-standard urban geometry capture these dynamics. As a digital city tool, space syntax enables the designer to understand spatial design effects and intervene appropriately at the micro/meso scale because the impact of the multiscale/speed private/public transport network interface with urban design is a vital component of pausing for sharing, matching and learning. However, motorised transport will become silent, pollutionless and driverless; speed differential and traffic volume will impact the quality of the experience of pausing. Figure 6 shows the potential of different spatial configurations. 'Offline, online' is an alternative to the privatisation of public space encountered in pods. At macro scale, social differentiation between radial/orbital and the mainly radial public transport network reinforces spatial inequity. Spatial justice is a multiscale spatial design project.

This is too brief an introduction to discuss every aspect of how space syntax spatial analyses enable spatial design economies. Already available and digitally mapped by this tool are residential, skills, education, income, potential expenditure and employment, local endowments and capacities, opportunities location, location and location profiles. The spatial designer, whether working as spatial policy-maker, transport or urban planner, or architect, can look anew at the multilayered interfaces of sharing, matching and learning, the multiscale/speed of transport and pausing; the multiscale non-standard geometric effects of city region layout design. Spatial design economies have the potential to coordinate urban and transport network design for the better by enhancing, matching, learning and sharing. ⚙

HYPERHABITAT

What are the possibilities and implications of global connectivity? Could individual living spaces be wired up to large-scale structures and networks? **Neil Leach** describes how Vicente Guallart's Hyperhabitat installation for the 2008 Venice Biennale engaged with these themes.

REPROGRAMMING THE WORLD

Vicente Guallart, Hyperhabitat: Reprogramming the World, Venice Biennale, 2008

opposite: The relations embraced by Hyperhabitat are purely physical – those that make functional interactions between things possible. Any node on the planet can be physically linked to any other by way of networks, such as water supply, sewage, energy, data, transportation of people or goods, and waste.

above: The nodes are functional accumulators that make it possible to carry out an activity. Anyone and everyone is welcome to install any individual object, building or place on the planet. A series of similar objects (for example, a series of books in a neighbourhood) can be installed in order to create a community of books for sharing.

Functional nodes are the places for creating proposals for reprogramming the world. Nodes of the same or different contents and scales can be connected. Users are invited to relate nodes in different 'habitats', whether created by themselves or by others, which may include their own or other people's nodes. The 'line codes' can include examples of ways of operating and acting in relation to proposals for reprogramming the world.

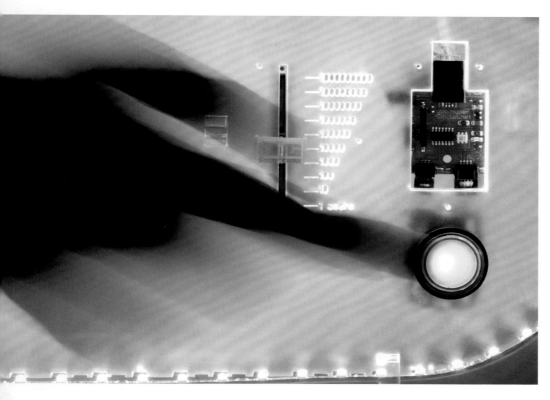

The line codes proposed in Hyperhabitat are essentially relationships posited in abstract form, and can be emotional or functional. They do not identify the kinds of relationships that are established directly between objects. Future implementations of the system will give more specific representations of these interactions.

In a world of global connectivity, we are hooked up in an information superhighway. We are all networked. But what does this mean in terms of the spaces of our everyday lives, our habitats? How are these spaces programmed within a globalised system?

Hyperhabitat: Reprogramming the World, an installation directed by Vicente Guallart for Venice Biennale in 2008, posited the need to reprogramme the structures with which we inhabit the world through the introduction of distributed intelligence in the nodes, networks and environments with which we construct buildings, cities and territories. It made visible the multiscalar relationships between each object and those on a higher scale (from the scale of an individual to that of our whole planet of 10 billion people), and displayed the 'line codes' that visitors were encouraged to propose. It also incorporated an Internet platform where visitors were invited to submit proposals for reprogramming the world by means of line codes that showed how relating things in different ways could result in urban systems that consume less energy and actively facilitate social interaction.

The installation involved the construction of a 1:1 scale replica of a floor of an apartment building with shared spaces being constructed in Gandia (Valencia), from the Sociopolis Sharing Tower. The furniture and appliances of the apartment were made of methacrylates with embedded microservers, which interacted with one another to generate relationships that were displayed as a large-format projection on which the line codes could be drawn to suggest relationships or between nodes. All of the objects in the house had an Internet 0 node – constituting the largest network of microservers assembled to date – with which they were directly interrelated with one another, just as neurons are in the brain.

Users were invited to create multiple habitats, spaces that related all of the possible functions that could be carried out in the world, on all possible scales: those of the neighbourhood, the city (useful for studying the urbanity of its relational form), the country or the planet. For a habitat to be operational, it was first necessary to upload nodes on multiple scales. A habitat could contain a specific set of objects, and be created to draw a line code to relate functional nodes.

Hyperhabitat: Reprogramming the World was a collaboration between Guallart Architects, the Institute for Advanced Architecture of Catalonia, MIT's Center for Bits and Atoms and the Bestiario software design consultancy. At a secondary level, then, the project articulated the forms of networking that are beginning to colonise architectural practice as a result of innovations in digital technology. Not only did it engage with advanced programming and digital fabrication in its design and construction; it also – in the very partnership forged to create it – expressed the forms of collaboration that have become increasingly prevalent within the building industry. In the highly digitised age of the 21st century, architecture has become so thoroughly enmeshed within a network of other disciplines that what we are witnessing are new hybrid, mutant forms of practice that serve to reinvent the discourse of architecture as we know it. ∆

Is the iPhone and a whole new generation of mobiles and PDAs eclipsing the physical city? Whereas once the metropolis alone brought together people, markets, goods, transport and information, the iPhone and similar handheld devices are changing spatial interaction. From Los Angeles, **Benjamin H Bratton** ruminates on the full impact of this technological shift.

An experiment: one-half of all architects and urbanists in the entire world should, as of now, stop designing new buildings and new developments altogether. Instead they should invest the historical depth and intellectual nuance of their architectural imaginations into the design and programming of new software that provides for the better use of structures and systems we already have. It is a simple matter of good content management. The other half, the control group, may continue as before.

Sitting in traffic on a Los Angeles freeway, looking at my edits for this essay, I am reminded of Joan Didion's revelation that this is the most authentic Angeleno social experience. We are not going to any place, all lined up behind our windshields, we are all already there.[1] Today, bumper to bumper, we are now all also on our phones and PDAs: taking meetings, texting, emailing, Googling, checking on this and that, editing essays on our iPhones. This is the home and office. We do not always need to arrive, because we are already there: if this was your home, you would live here by now. This is a grid that segments and enables an inertial sort of mobility. Ensconced in our furtive provisional networks, the car is no longer the primary technology of mobility, even in LA. It has gone the way of the building. By the time Reyner Banham arrived, the car had eaten LA; now the phone is eating the car.

The 'mobile' began life as a 'car phone', but now the terms are reversed. In The Transformers,[2] the alien robot became a car, and the phone became a robot. Here now, the car becomes a phone. As mobility has transformed from mechanical to informational, the car is augmented by hands-free telephony, Bluetooth networks, in-dash GPS navigation systems offering visualised or spoken directions, iPod jacks, big screens counting down the drops of fuel while talking to you in weird accents, and emergency concierge communications by built-in satellite

intercom. The handset does all this too, steering us in different directions by maps, recommendations, search results, geotags and so forth. The phone and car find ways to subcontract each other's functions, one to the other and back again.

In ways that would have made no sense in Banham's LA, the car's interfaciality is an important criterion of performance as a personal vehicle. In addition to the slow move to alternative power, the clearest change to the car in the last five years is in the display electronics within its primary interface, the dashboard/cockpit. If the grille on the outside used to be the car's face – its look – now the face comes with the voice on the inside. That new primary, brandable experience interface does not focus on how a car looks in the world, but on how the world looks gazing out through the lens of the car. The car+phone hybrid is a mass medium, a mobile cinema+micro-urbanism for one driver/user, a habitat organised and narrated by data networks. But in the end, they are not equal; the handset is the ascendant vehicle, and the car is the architecture in slow disappearance.

Programming Gestures Programming Space

No one, today, can know what the city of tomorrow will be. One part of the semantic wealth which belonged to it in the past … it will lose that, certainly … The creative and formative role of the city will be taken charge of by other communications systems … their vocabulary and syntax, consciously and deliberately.
Juliette, in Jean-Luc Godard's *Two or Three Things I Know About Her* (1967)[3]

How can we properly theorise the digital at the scale of the city, and the city rendered as digital media? First, it is not really about newness. Foundational, even primal conditions are now reanimated (layering effects, invisible information made visible, physical computation, collapsed distances, remote control, etc) that cannot be reduced to a new digital sheen on an old analogue world. I think of Sanford Kwinter's allegory of the digital Pleistocene.[4] Humans, as a species,

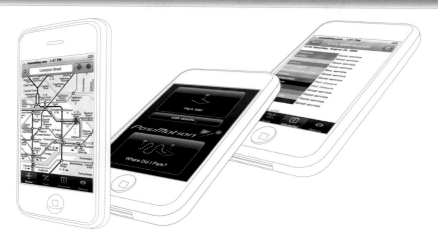

have evolved little in the last hundred thousand years, and hardly at all since the appearance of writing. Our senses, our inherited built-in media, are the same as those that allowed us to survive the predatory rhythms of the primordial savannah; and in the city's very real landscape of information production and reception those same rhythms persist, in communication with our new media and augmented cognition. Architecture is at least partially tuned to these. The Modernist call for a more intense technologisation of the disciplinary *doxa*, blending urban and cybernetic programs, is a now permanent feature of the discourse.[5] Any such programming of this perceptual space casts the digital city as a shared nervous system, and today the rupture of digital information networks through the membrane of the city into the open view of people and their mobile screens relies on the body's capacity to 'proprioceptively' map its own displacement in real and imagined geographies.[6]

Peter Sloterdijk's historical image of environmental embodiment, an irreducible, self-animating circuit of habit and habitat, pertains equally to the ambient informational fields that cloud the city and through which we learn to mediate spaces both near and far.[7] But such spheres need to be learned and, while it takes time to master remote controls, let alone the control of remoteness, we are fast learners. There is a monkey at Duke University who, through interfacial electronics connected to his brain, controls a robotic arm miles away.[8] His dispositional impulses become informational pulses which, properly mediated, effect a remote prosthesis to do his bidding. Like this monkey's, our own bodies are infused and intersected by the extensional networks of the living city, both controlling its machinery at a distance and triangulated socially and psychologically by that machinery in the course of our movements. We

learn to operate the city as a meta-interface, one comprised of many smaller tactical interfaces (just as we learned QWERTY, internalising the feedback of expression and inscription as a physical interface to the production of written language).

Substances at Hand

If the first function of the city is proximity (to people, markets, goods, transport, information), the smart digital handset condenses the city itself into an extensible software+hardware platform. Globally more people own mobile phones than regularly access the Web, and for most of the world their first computer will be a handheld one that is also a mobile phone. Computation will not arrive as a desk-bound or even lap-bound experience, but as an active network linking speech to data for ambulant gesturing bodies moving through active worlds.[9] Phone+city is a composite read-write medium, allowing for real-time communication through multiple modes, now and in situ, and represents, in combination, an important infrastructure of any emergent global democratic society. It can do this not only because it enables physical, communicative and thereby social mobility, but because it dramatically reinserts specific location into digital space and does so by making location gestural.

The foremost infrastructural projects of our generation have been the planetary proliferation of digital information networks, and now another that moves that infrastructure from an embedded *sous*-terrestrial network to a pervasive in-hand circuit of body and information cloud. Computation evolves from a rare, expensive national asset to a cheap ubiquitous vapour. That stream's orifice is the handheld phone, PDA, homing beacon, Geiger counter, magic antenna, virtual goggles, scanning X-ray filter, field recording microphone and camera that makes hidden wisdom appear; the device becomes a window on to the hidden layers of data held in or about the user's immediate environment. Urban and network diagrams are images now animated in hand, transformed from maps into image-instruments with which to connect and control the immediate and remote environment. Both distance and nearness erode under the weight of the interface's imagery.[10]

The iPhone is the first to put it all together in a way that changes how a critical mass of consumers could envision a new genre of computing: interaction-in-the-wild. The impact of this as a new mode of spatial interaction has yet to be realised. The iPhone is not close to being the most popular mobile and is not likely to be any time soon. At the time of writing, Apple has sold about 13 million iPhones in total, whereas Nokia sells more than a million phones per day. Research in Motion's Blackberry has done far more to put the office desktop in workers' pockets. But the impact of the iPhone outweighs its comparative success as a product. Unlike its competitors, the iPhone does not feel like a desktop or phone experience, but instead something immediately recognisable as a personal interface to ambient information. The shift from point-and-click to multitouch gesturing represents a 'substantialisation' of data, a cognitive shift in the 'how' but also the 'what'. Compared to other devices it does not so much present icons that mimic other things and trigger 'virtual' events as it is embodied by tangible interfaces activating living information in the here and now. It shifts thinking from interfaces that arrange pictures of things to an interface full of actual data substances you can directly grab and manipulate.

The hardware itself makes this possible. Enclosed in sensate glass, the iPhone interface and hardware blend into what the user perceives as a single dynamic form or field. Framed in this way, 'apps' have their own 'thingness' that similar applications on other devices do not. Others have menus and contextual options but suggest no immediate tangibility. The iPhone graphical user interface (GUI) is filled with things not metaphors; it is a tactile movie shell to be pushed and pulled as real, rubbery stuff which seems illuminated from within, not as a layer but as an organic expression; it has 'faciality'. This tangibility and anthropomorphology are what makes it work, socially and psychologically, as an interface to the world directly, not to the network indirectly – to the real, not to the iconic.

The Turing City and the Protocols of Program[11]

The city as seen through the medium of that face oozes with living data to be touched and rewritten all over again. Interaction with this information is recursive; action taken with it on a micro level is itself new information that in turn informs what everyone else sees on a macro level. In this recursion the presence of the information, good or bad, can be directly disruptive to social behaviour as people change their paths and decisions in the image of

the actions and swerves of others they see indexed in their at-hand interfaces. The graphical appearance of this interface, then, is less a figural representation than a direct urban event, part of bigger circuits of concrete movement. Thus for the architect, the digital city becomes a habitat, a sphere in Sloterdijk's sense, to the extent that it becomes the foundational layer of the designable software stack.

This portends to both radically complicate and simplify architectural and urban programming strategies. Architectural program and interfaces can reside in structure or furniture, fixed or unfixed.[12] The same is true for software and the Turing City, where program becomes less ordered and more entropic, always shuttling between mobile and immobile interfaces. 'Program' can be understood as modes of the social that require some supporting material culture to repeat themselves, and which were traditionally zoned within partitioned locations. Now as the work of that material is more available to the calculations of software, the program itself is as portable as the handset which, for one or many users, projects and transposes a program into a given locale at a given time. The principle: much of what we, as a society, used to ask of architecture in the functional organisation of people and organisations in space and time, we now ask of software. Is software, in-hand, less an augmentation of a situation than the physical environment as a layer of a software/hardware stacked network? In the case of the iPhone, program is less about geography and more about opportunity. As urban 'functions' are translated and transposed into applications, they can be activated alone or in groups at a moment's notice, providing a different interface to the same location and through this a specific urban program, one likely co-occupying that location with many others.

Locative media pose integrative design questions. Software program, architectural program (and political program) mix and merge in new ways. Architecture's programming expertise must participate wholeheartedly in this assignment, replicating, condensing, mobilising, diverging and converging the small and large interfaces that constitute the social. This is less the design of the network than of the computational mechanisms that formulate the nodal and edge conditions and the interfaces that provide the access to, or protection of, these. It is both meticulously mechanical and broadly dramaturgical, a systematising of the possibility of particular events appearing, both on schedule and off, and of the scenarios by which those events become residual social languages. It is a geo-computational program, but one that calculates conditions of appearance more than it scripts or contains what finally emerges. The design frameworks are protocols that ensure a predictable malleability of information flow. For example, the street grid is a protocol, a dumb fixed standard that allowed the modern city to emerge as a dynamic network. If it had been animate or idiosyncratic it would not mediate the maximal churn that it does. Taken to its radical logic, Archizoom's No-Stop City was a rendering of this modernity in its purified form – the city as an infinite protocol. In this, the integrative programming of inherited urban modernities converges and competes with new protocols that afford the design of overlapping geographies and concurrent assemblages, protocols with names like Geo RSS, GML, GPX, KML, EXIF and Geo OpenSearch. An urban ecology of software continues to emerge and here the concern is not what the iPhone (or any product) per se will allow, but whether all and any allowable platforms will support the promiscuous multiplication of loquacious protocols.

As the channels of the city are compressed and revealed by the handset's interfaces, the gravity and contiguity of architectural programs dissolve. Use is always mixed. The Turing City requires a logic of program that is less like an OMA sectional diagram and more like the iPhone deck itself. The sectional stacking of many discrete zones of behaviour into a single envelope gives way to interior and exterior sites that can be activated in any number of different ways by different people using different software in-hand. The same is true of the urban scale. For the traditional urban zoning project, the rhythm of programmatic (social, behavioural) discontinuity is dense, but each is bound to its restricted zone in planimetric or sectional space. In the Turing City, 'zoning' becomes a more problematic technique. In the traditional sense, it becomes less enforceable, and even self-defeating, when a whole section of the city interacts differently with a user or group depending on what software they are running. Ten minutes later, a different software activates a different program, and in this architecture is to some extent relieved of the programmatic responsibility of functional instrumentality or even specific purpose. All these spatial logistics have been outsourced to much more liquid media.

Protocols are the grammar, but the architecture of the software stack is the real framing possibility of program for designers. On the go, this is really a GeoStack, a set of tools that create and use the data of the geographically intelligent Web, designing and tracing information from its point of creation through publication, sharing, aggregation and, finally, consumption. The stack's verticality is an arrangement of relationally open and closed channels of information production, manipulation and accessibility. Plumbing into plumbing. Through this, designers designate where to place their services, identify synergies and develop extensible systems that can enhance their particular offerings. The range of services and opportunities for savvy urbanists is vast: location-aware augmented reality viewfinders, macro-sensing and reality-mining of composite crowd-sourced behavioural

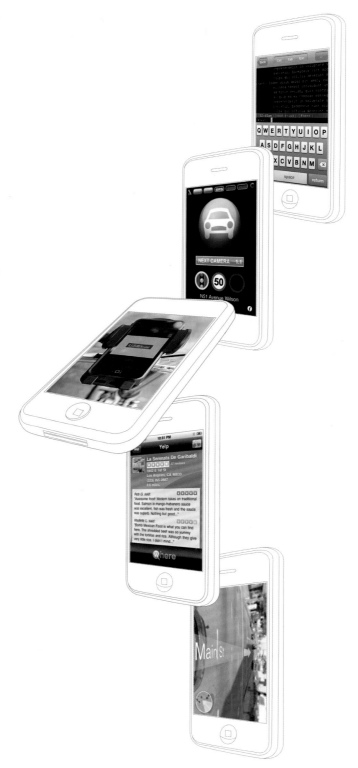

data, citizen activists using GIS and mass-market Geobrowsers and plugging open map layers into their Ruby and MySQL applications, real-time disease outbreak visualisation and real-time micro governance of biopolitical swarms, traffic control sensor and tollbooth hacks, individually reconfigurable interior partitions, collapsing rooms and even floors, proprietary parking applications, post-Twitter ones keeping us always at the tent-pole centre of our concentric and now minutely reflexive social network, bus bench RSS feeds, pigeons that blog, lifelong syncing of car-phone-home-clouds, in-pocket web servers, real-time traffic, congestion and crime data patterns informing personal routeware, point-and-scan barcode readers, 4.5-inch Bloomberg terminals, instant carbon-footprint visualisation, real-time voice-to-voice language translations, location-based serial cinema, Google Habitat, real-time cab spotting, personal arphid managers, data-privacy consulting services, grey-market concierges and so on, all posted with at least partially open application programming interfaces (APIs) enabling other applications to further build on the existing stacks.

A Small Onyx Frame of Immanence

It is said that at the end of the rainbow there is a pot of gold. Where that end is, however poses a problem, since it is different for every observer. The rainbow is actually a distorted virtual image of the sun. Nevertheless, it looks like a real object. Could it be that similar distortions apply to other 'real' objects?
From Otto E Rossler and Peter Weibel, 'Endophysics of Our Rainbow World', 1992[13]

Regarding further briefing details for my future software assignment to the one-half of architects: any such development is fraught with risk, not only because of what it would leave behind but because of what it might accomplish and quickly lose ability to control. The experimental half turning its attention to the Turing City should consider the several conditions (or admonitions) below. First of all, this represents an activation of human-object networks in ways that are both new and primordial. Anticipate the rapid co-evolution of urban behaviour and urban software, such that the devices themselves and their capacities will appear to be evolving more in relation to each other than to us. This Darwinism of the device will make it seem as though we are their media and not the other way around. Appearances can be factual. In this the explosion of hyperlocal and hypervisual information will both amplify and multiply the intensities of social interaction, but will also reveal the complexity of communication between non-humans (animals, ecologies, infrastructures). Just as our collective urban cognition comes online it will be exposed as a hopelessly outflanked minority discourse. Quite clearly the computational intensification of the interface will make it more and more cinematic, and more affectively factual, effectively exacerbating everything we already know about the instability of cinematic memory, action, projection, repetition and pixellation, and bringing these deeper into everyday life.

The social-psychological results of all this will be complex and contradictory. Pervasive computing will make inanimate objects see, hear and comment on our interactions with them. This experience will, in many cases, be indistinguishable from a psychotic break, or from the affinity rituals of classical animism. In a recent interview, Paul Virilio notes that today's qualities of technology – instantaneity, ubiquity, immediacy – are those associated with the divine. The killer application of pervasive computing is not advertising to the hipster *flâneur*; it is religion, and its impact on Abrahamic monotheisms will be turbulent, existential and fertile. The iPhone City is post-secular.[14] **Δ**

Notes

Thank you to Bruna Mori for her excellent edits.

1. Interview with Joan Didion in *Shotgun Freeway: Drives Through Lost LA*, documentary film by Morgan Neville and Harry Pallenberg, 1995.
2. *The Transformers*. Michael Bay. 143 min. USA release date 2 July 2007.
3. *2 ou 3 Choses que Je Sais d'Elle* (*Two or Three Things I Know About Her*). Jean-Luc Godard. 85 min. France release date 17 March 1967.
4. Sanford Kwinter, 'Digital Pleistocene', Seminar description, SCI-Arc, Los Angeles, summer 2008. An excerpt: 'The contemporary "mediascape" has given such primacy of place to communication that it has transformed it into substance itself, the very material of which we, and our world, are made. Yet all biological substance is founded on signaling, from the first single-cell organisms nearly 3 billion years ago to the most sophisticated forms of human social life (MySpace?) today. There is no family of animal that is not defined by its capacities for signaling and no ecological niche that is not defined by the infrastructure that supports this signaling. When the human line broke off from its ape ancestors it was a result of a new capacity for communication (a new hand-eye-brain-mouth machine) and the rise of a new signaling niche in the environment to be filled (the long distance savannah).'
5. Throughout this essay, the US 'program' is used to indicate both architectural 'programme' (English spelling) as well as computational 'program'. It is precisely the promiscuous ambiguity between one and the other that the author wishes to convey. After the appearance of the computer but before the mobile phone, Reyner Banham called for a revolution in the technologisation of the environment, a complete folding of architectural and cybernetic programs/programmes. Reyner Banham, 'Architecture After 1960', *Architectural Review* 127, No 755, April 1960, pp 253–60. See also Anthony Vidler, 'Toward a Theory of Architectural Program', *October* 106, Fall 2003, pp 59–74.
6. See Brian Massumi, 'Sensing the Virtual, Building the Insensible', in *AD Hypersurface Architecture*, August 1998, pp 16–25.
7. Peter Sloterdijk, *Sphären Bde.1-3: Eine Trilogie: 3 Bände*, Suhrkamp (Frankfurt), 11 November 2008.
8. See http://www.pratt.duke.edu/news/?id=753. Accessed 15 November 2008.
9. By comparison, One Laptop Per Child (Nicholas Negroponte's attempt to distribute inexpensive, highly functional laptops designed for the needs of children in the developing world) cannot possibly keep pace with the exponential multiplication of increasingly sophisticated handsets. Compare it with the reach of Nokia, the world's largest handset manufacturer and mobile software provider, selling 1.34 million devices per day. Nokia generally develops its own software for its own phones, but has a strong interest in the reality of pervasive computing as a global social platform. The work done by its researchers, such as Jan Chipchase, Younghee Jung, Adam Greenfield, Julian Bleecker and Rebecca Allen, attests to this investment. See http://research.nokia.com/research.
10. See Benjamin H Bratton and Natalie Jeremijenko, *Suspicious Images, Latent Interfaces*, Architectural League of New York, September 2008. This pamphlet also deals with information visualisation and ecological monitoring through these problematics. See http://www.situatedtechnologies.net/?q=node/88.
11. Perhaps a better name for the more general condition of urban cultures reconfigured around pervasive computing would draw on the figure of that great computational ontologist, Alan Turing.
12. A program of illumination can come from a window (architecture) or a lamp (furniture), sitting from a chair or a fold in the wall, cooling from a walk-in freezer or a refrigerator, and so on. The designation of which programs are fixed and which are unfixed, architecture or furniture, is always very open even if not normally appreciated as such.
13. Otto E Rossler and Peter Weibel, 'Endophysics of Our Rainbow World' in Karl Gerbel and Peter Weibel (eds), *The World from Within – ENDO & NANO*, Veritas-Verlag (Linz), 1992, pp 13–21. Also republished in Peter Weibel (ed), *Olafur Eliasson: Surroundings Surrounded – Essays on Space and Science*, MIT Press (Cambridge, MA), 2001, p 504.
14. The Mumbai terror attacks of November 2008 occurred four days after completion of the first draft of this essay, and the writing of these horrifically verified concluding remarks. In the days just following, we learned about the array of powerful but off-the-shelf navigation and communications software and hardware used by the attackers to coordinate their movements throughout multiple locations at once: satellite phones, handheld GPS, anonymised email, Google Earth, voice-to-text software, and so on. On 16 October 2008 the US army published a report considering scenarios in which terrorists would coordinate urban mobilisation using Twitter. See http://www.fas.org/irp/eprint/mobile.pdf. In Mumbai, Twitter was used by hostages and others to report and share information on the events in real time. The #Mumbai hash tag generated hundreds of pages of texts. See http://twitter.com/Mumbai.

Illustrations by Lindsay Noble, CHK Design. Art direction: Christian Küsters, CHK Design

Contributors

Hernan Diaz Alonso is the principal and founder of Xefirotarch, an award-winning design firm specialising in architecture, product and digital motion with practices in Los Angeles. He currently teaches full-time studio design and visual studies, and is the thesis coordinator at SCI-Arc, design studio professor at the GSAPP at Columbia, and a professor at the Universität für Angewandte Kunst Wien.

Michael Batty is Bartlett Professor of Planning at University College London where he directs the Centre for Advanced Spatial Analysis (CASA). His research work involves the development of computer models of cities and regions, focusing on urban morphology and dynamics, the most recent being *Cities and Complexity* (MIT Press, 2005). He is editor of the journal *Environment and Planning B: Planning and Design*, and a Fellow of the British Academy. He was awarded a CBE in the Queen's Birthday Honours in June 2004.

Benjamin H Bratton is Associate Professor of Visual Arts at UC San Diego, and directs the design policy programme at CALIT2, at the University of California, San Diego. He has also taught at the Southern California Institute of Architecture since 2001. He is a principal of The Culture Industry, a multidisciplinary design research consultancy that helps large organisations plan for the overlaps of physical and computational spaces. His research, writing and practical interests include contemporary social theory, the perils and potentials of pervasive computing, architectural theory and provocation, inverse brand theory, software studies, systems design and development, and the spatial rhetorics of exceptional violence.

Alain Chiaradia is an architect and urbanist based in London. He is an honorary Senior Research Fellow of the Bartlett School of Architecture, University College London; Cities Programme Studio Tutorial Fellow at the London School of Economics and Political Science; a co-founder of Chora, an institute for architecture and urbanism; and an executive research director at Space Syntax Ltd, where he has led spatial design and research projects. He recently led the Intangible Values of Urban Layout – the largest project for the UCL-Urbanbuzz: Building Sustainable Communities knowledge exchange programme funded by the Higher Education Funding Council for England, Higher Education Innovation Fund and Department for Innovation, Universities and Skills. One phase of the project involved the production of the first megacity region spatial values map covering the Greater Southeast of England.

Manuel DeLanda is the author of five philosophy books: *War in the Age of Intelligent Machines* (Zone Books, 1991); *A Thousand Years of Nonlinear History* (Zone Books, 1997); *Intensive Science and Virtual Philosophy* (Continuum, 2002); *A New Philosophy of Society* (Continuum, 2006); and *Philosophy, Emergence and Simulation* (2009). He teaches two seminars at the University of Pennsylvania, Department of Architecture: 'Philosophy of History: Theories of Self-Organization and Urban Dynamics' and 'Philosophy of Science: Thinking about Structures and Materials'.

Vicente Guallart works at the confluence of architecture, nature and new technologies. Based in Spain, his projects include the Denia Mountain, three ports in northern Taiwan, the Sociopolis neighbourhood in Valencia and the Cultural Gates to Alborz in Teheran. He is a director of the Institute for Advanced Architecture of Catalonia (Iaac) in Barcelona. His work has been presented in several international venues, and he has recently published his latest book, *Geologics: Geography, Bits and Architecture* (Actar, 2009).

Neil Leach is Professor of Architectural Theory at the University of Brighton, and visiting professor at the University of Southern California. He has also taught at the Architectural Association, Columbia GSAPP, Cornell University, Dessau Institute of Architecture and SCI-Arc. He is the author, editor and translator of many books, including *Rethinking Architecture* (Routledge 1997), *The Anaesthetics of Architecture* (MIT Press, 1999), *Designing for a Digital World* (John Wiley & Sons, 2002) and *Digital Tectonics* (John Wiley & Sons, 2004), and was co-curator of the '(Im)material Processes: New Digital Techniques for Architecture' exhibition at the Architecture Biennial Beijing in 2008.

R&Sie(n) is a Paris-based architectural office set up in 1989 and led by **François Roche** and Stéphanie Lavaux. Roche has held professorships at the Bartlett School of Architecture, Upenn, Columbia GSAPP and the University of Applied Arts, Vienna. The firm's projects have been exhibited at Columbia University, UCLA, the ICA, Mori Art Museum, Centre Pompidou, SF Moma, MAM, MIT's Media Lab, Tate Modern and Orléans/ArchiLab International. R&Sie(n) was among those architects selected by France for the 1990, 1996, 2000 and 2002 Venice Architectural Biennale, and was also featured in the international selections for 2000, 2004 and 2008.

Patrik Schumacher is a partner at and senior designer for Zaha Hadid Architects, working on projects including MAXXI: National Centre of Contemporary Art and Architecture in Rome, the BMW Central Building in Leipzig and the Dubai Opera House. He studied architecture at the University of Stuttgart and at Southbank University in London. He completed his architectural diploma and received his DiplIng. from Stuttgart University in 1990, and in 1999 received his DrPhil from the Institute for Cultural Sciences at the University of Klagenfurt. He has been a co-director of the Design Research Laboratory at the Architectural Association School of Architecture since 1996, and co-taught a series of postgraduate option studios with Zaha Hadid at the University of Illinois in Chicago, at Columbia University and at the Harvard Graduate School of Design.

Peter Trummer is an architect and researcher based in Amsterdam. He is Head of the Associative Design Research Program at the Berlage Institute in Rotterdam. He received his Masters degree from the Technical University in Graz and completed his postgraduate studies at the Berlage Institute in Amsterdam in 1997. He was previously a project architect at UN Studio, and a co-founder of Offshore Architects before establishing his own practice in 2004. In 2007 he was guest professor at the Technical University in Munich. He lectures and teaches internationally, at institutions including the Berlage Institute, the AA, University for Applied Art, UCLA and SCI-Arc, and at Rice University in Houston. His essays have been published in journals including *Arch+* and *Volume*.

Tom Verebes is an architect, researcher and educator. He co-directed the Design Research Lab (DRL) at the Architectural Association in London until 2009, where he taught design studios and seminars in the post-professional MArch course from 1997. He is currently associate professor in the Faculty of Architecture at the University of Hong Kong, and was previously a visiting professor at ABK Stuttgart. In 1995 he co-founded the OCEAN design network, subsequently directed OCEAN UK as a node of oceanD, and is currently Creative Director of OCEAN.CN, a consultancy network based in Hong Kong. He has written, published, exhibited and lectured extensively in Europe, North America, Asia and the Middle East.

C O N T E N T S

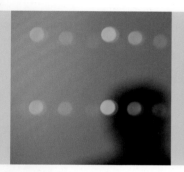

JAN KAPLICKÝ (1937–2009)

Homage to an Extraordinary Life of Unfulfilled Dreams and Major Successes

Jan Kaplický
(18 April 1937–14 January 2009)

Future Systems, National
Library of the Czech
Republic, Prague, Czech
Republic, 2007

Jan Kaplický's visionary work for Future Systems was some of the most imaginative and inspiring of the last few decades. His passion and excitement for architecture exudes through such remarkable forms as the Lord's Media Centre and Selfridges in Birmingham. It was also effectively disseminated through his publications: most notably the *For Inspiration Only* picture books that he produced for Wiley-Academy in the late 1990s. A staunch believer in the power of books and journals, he was a loyal supporter of *AD* and an editorial board member for many years; always generous with his time and willing to express his ideas candidly. Here, close friend and fellow Czech architect and writer **Ivan Margolius,** celebrates not only Kaplický the architect, but also the extraordinary life and sensibility of the man behind his work.

True friendship relies on trust, understanding and mutual respect. Since Jan and I first came across each other in the 1980s, our affinity and rapport grew and deepened. We met in the offices of YRM (Yorke Rosenberg Mardall) in London, where I was working, and Jan was invited to collaborate on the Terminal 5 competition entry. Having both been in exile, we shared similar life histories and situations: starting again, living on our own in a foreign

> 'He will never be here again; neither will he be absent. I have sacrificed his place at my table, as a useless illusion, but in his death he remains my real friend.'
>
> Antoine de Saint-Exupéry, *Lettre à un Otage*, 1943

country. We came from Prague, were our parents' single offspring, and had common interests and passions. My parents suffered during the Second World War and the Communist era. Both of them were interned in concentration camps, and then my father, Rudolf Margolius, was executed after the infamous Slánský Trial in November 1952. Jan's father, Josef Kaplický, a painter, sculptor and professor at Prague Academy of Fine Arts, passed away suddenly in February 1962 after being hounded by the Communist authorities, particularly by Deputy Prime Minister Václav Kopecký, a vicious Party hatchet man, for not conforming to the prescribed Stalinist art doctrines. I left Czechoslovakia in 1966 wanting to forget the past and begin again, and Jan was forced to leave two years later after the Soviet occupation. There was no future in Communist Czechoslovakia for either of us.

Jan was born in Prague in 1937 during a turbulent period of Czech history. This was the year before the Munich Conference, which decreed the surrender of the Bohemian and Moravian border territories. Then the occupation of the remnant of Czechoslovakia by the Third Reich came in March 1939. Jan lived with his parents in a house at Pod vyhlídkou 5 in the beautiful Ořechovka district of Prague, close to the Villa Müller (1930), designed by Adolf Loos, which was to become by his choice a pivotal building in his life. He visited the villa with his parents as a child, he was married there, and even his funeral was held there. Jan's artistic genes were moulded by his father's creative endeavours and complemented by the ability of his mother Jiřina who was a skilful book illustrator.

During his childhood walks with his parents through his native city he encountered and witnessed the signs of brutal Nazi occupation, the Jewish transports, the Gestapo raids, the arrests of Czechoslovak civilians especially after Reinhard Heydrich's assassination by the Czechoslovak partisans in May 1942. But what he had also seen was the military machinery of the time: tanks,

Future Systems, Hauer King House, Islington, London, 1992
Created around existing trees, this London town house beautifully contrasts nature with man-made, late 20th-century architecture.

Future Systems, Marshall-Andrews House, Pembrokeshire, Wales, 1994
Fully set into the coastal landscape, this weekend retreat house has a glazed 'eye' that turns towards the sea.

**Future Systems, Selfridges Department
Store, Birmingham, 1999**
The facade treatment of spun
aluminium discs for this inward-looking
building became an instant Birmingham
icon and was chosen to illustrate a
Royal Mail postage stamp.

Future Systems, Lord's NatWest Media Centre, Marylebone Cricket Club, London, 1994
The inspiration for the RIBA Stirling Prize–winning media stand at Lord's Cricket Ground was a photographic camera capturing the sporting events with its lens. The construction exploited the semi-monocoque shell structure derived from boat-building techniques.

armoured cars, weapons and aeroplanes – and for a small boy these were powerful images. The potent outdoor pictures were complemented by a peaceful family life where Jan was surrounded by his parents' avant-garde book and magazine collection, tinplate toys, Greyhound bus and Schüco cars, a Fröbel wooden-block building kit and a Merkur (Czech version of Meccano) construction set. Jan made models of boats and aeroplanes, and observed his parents at work. The Kaplickýs' house was furnished with Bauhaus metal tube chairs, tables and sofas. Important Czech artists came to visit, including painter Jan Zrzavý, sculptor Bedřich Stefan, photographer Josef Sudek and architect Pavel Smetana. All these activities influenced and inspired Jan, initiating his dreams for a brighter future.

After the war and the liberation by the Soviets, a new era began. For Jan the new freedom was heralded by Josef Havlíček's and Karel Honzík's Prague Pension Institute building (1933), which had been cleaned of its war-khaki camouflage paint revealing the original bright-beige ceramic tile facades. Jan started his education at Hana Benešová School, a functionalist building erected in the 1930s, in Pohořelec, a suburb of Prague. It had a large glass front, balconies and terraces, and plywood-seat metal tube furniture inside. Jan explored every detail and found beauty in the objects and buildings around him.

In 1948 the Communist Party took over the government, the free democracy was toppled and the country came under totalitarian Stalinist domination. Communist propaganda encouraged by Soviet policies kept on attacking personal freedom and artistic creativity, limiting development, stopping access to Western culture and restricting travel abroad. Subscriptions to magazines such as *Life* were cancelled and the Kaplický family lost touch with the outside world. Luckily Jan's godfather, Dr Josef Brumlík, who lived in the US, managed to send several books and magazines on architecture. Jan rediscovered famous pre-war Czech culture and designs: the music of Jaroslav Ježek, films by Jiří Voskovec and Jan Werich, and Tatra streamlined automobiles. He admired Ludvík Kysela's Baťa building (1929), Pavel Janák's Juliš Hotel (1933), Oldřich Tyl's Trade Fair building (1928) and Jaromír Krejcar's Paris Czechoslovak Exhibition Pavilion (1937). Jan visited the innovative town of Zlín and marvelled at the early Romanesque and Gothic churches in the Bohemian countryside. The greatest influence, though, was the military defence bunkers erected along the Czechoslovak border, based on the French example of the Maginot Line in about 1935. The way their concrete curved forms fitted cosily into the Czech meadows and forests caught Jan's imagination.

Between 1956 and 1962 Jan studied architecture at the Academy of Fine Arts in Prague, where Czech architects Jan Smetana and Jan Sokol were his teachers. In 1959 he travelled to Moscow to explore Constructivist architecture and visited the national US exposition

Future Systems, National Library of the Czech Republic, Prague, Czech Republic, 2007
The controversial Future Systems' winning entry for the new 40,000-square-metre (430,560-square-foot) National Library of the Czech Republic, renamed by the Czechs as '*chobotnice*' (octopus), is situated within the green parkland of the Letná Plain in Prague. The site overlooks the city from above on a similarly high level to Prague Castle although it is hidden by trees. The aerial view confirms the important in-line juxtaposition of the library with the famous Renaissance Belvedere Royal Summerhouse and Prague Castle with St Vitus Cathedral. Prague's baroque buildings inspired the library's form, tint and curvature. The building is covered with champagne-coloured anodised aluminium tiles fading from a darker hue at the bottom to a lighter shade at the top. Circular windows distributed over the external undulated skin provide natural light for the mauve-coloured interior. The 10 million books, stored underground, are distributed to readers in less than 5 minutes by an innovative automated storage and retrieval system. Jan wanted the building to be lively and vibrant, and apart from the main library spaces and the public walkway running through the building, allowing easy access, the most significant areas were the top-level viewing platform and rendezvous café with its 'eye' vista over Prague. To Jan's consternation, Czech politicians, Czech architects and local public opinion found the design alien to their vision of Prague. The project continues to be debated and its future remains uncertain. Jan's supporters and friends are hopeful that the library, perhaps his most daring design, will eventually be constructed.

Future Systems, Antonín Dvořák Concert and Congress Centre Project, Čtyři Dvory, České Budějovice, Czech Republic, 2008
The proposal for the Antonín Dvořák Concert and Congress Centre sits on an old disused military site at Čtyři Dvory in the Czech town of České Budějovice, famous as the home town of Budvar beer. It consists of a foyer and two concert halls: the philharmonic hall seating 1,000 people, and the chamber music hall with 400 seats. Each hall displays a large rear window – a popular Future Systems feature – behind the performers that allows open views into the parkland behind the building. The spaces are shaped in free-form curves that aim to combine aesthetics with outstanding acoustic quality. In the Czech Republic, for its obvious shape and colour, the building was soon nicknamed '*rejnok*' (ray) after the elegantly formed seawater fish that had been the building's inspiration. The South Bohemian Society of Friends of Music hopes to build the centre despite Jan's untimely passing.

where he saw Richard Buckminster Fuller's houses, Charles Eames' furniture and American automobiles.

During his studies Jan set up a small practice and realised one apartment interior (1958), a garden ramp design (1965), the Franz Kafka memorial plaque (1966) and a small house design (1967), which was completed after he left the country in the summer of 1968, a few days after the Soviet Union occupied Czechoslovakia on 21 August.

After arriving in London Jan worked for Denys Lasdun, with Piano & Rogers on the Centre Pompidou and with Foster Associates on the Hong Kong Shanghai Bank. He met David Nixon first at Foster's office in 1972, and later at Louis de Soissons' practice. In 1979 they set up a consultancy: Future Systems. What initiated their thinking was a deep conviction that contemporary outdated building methods needed to advance to keep pace with progress in aerospace and electronics technologies. David Nixon moved to

California and Jan remained in London, though they continued to collaborate and design responsive buildings reflecting their new, innovative, lightweight engineering ideas. Buckminster Fuller, Charles Eames and Jean Prouvé became their father figures.

Although Jan disliked the word 'technology', his creativity continued to be influenced by innovative transport design up to the end of the 1980s: by cars, aeroplanes, boats and spacecraft. He loved the detail of the Czech Jawa motorcycle headlight housing moulded together with the front fork (1946) and the form of the Tatraplan car (1947), which he wanted to borrow from me and park in his office to inspire his staff. The monocoque skin, a frameless structural shell construction, and its transfer into architecture developed into Future Systems' central passion. In this way, building materials were used most economically, efficiently and in the most elegant way. Kaplický and Nixon were determined, and became optimistic about 'tomorrow's possibilities'. Many amazing designs were produced, but remained on paper.

In the late 1980s, when Jan joined forces in both his private life and practice with Amanda Levete, his interest turned to inspiration from nature, to organic free-flowing forms, plants, animals, fish and

Future Systems, Antonín Dvořák
Concert and Congress Centre Project,
Čtyři Dvory, České Budějovice, Czech
Republic, 2008
Philharmonic hall interior.

seashells. He felt that this source provided more opportunity to express his design ideas. His buildings became intelligent 'eyes', looking, observing, from inside to outside. He published several books on inspiration using unusual causes found in the world around us. He wanted to inspire young people, to explore, question and find beauty in ordinary objects. With Amanda's help, Future Systems became more commercially successful; they built several houses in London and in the countryside, and designed and realised the Media Centre for Lord's Cricket Ground (1994), which was awarded the Stirling Prize in 1999, the Floating Bridge (1994) in London's Docklands, and Selfridges Department Store (1999) in Birmingham. Their son Josef was born in 1995. Jan was delighted and honoured even with minor successes, for example, when the Royal Mail issued a 44 pence stamp showing Selfridges to commemorate Modern architecture in the UK. He boasted with a smile that his stamp was more valuable than the 30 pence Fosters' one.

In later years his designs turned to projects in the Czech Republic. The practice won the National Library competition in Prague (2007), the Antonín Dvořák Concert and Congres Centre (2008) was planned in České

Budějovice, and the Clubhouse Volavka and Villa Kaplický (2008) at Konopiště Resort, where private clients also wanted to have their houses built. His return to his homeland brought the break-up of his first marriage. In 2007 Jan married Eliška Fuchsová, a Czech film producer, and their daughter Johana was born on the day Jan died.

People who did not know Jan intimately perceived him as a man of pessimistic, gloomy and fatalistic outlook. This was far removed from his true nature. Czechs are sensitive people who suffered for centuries, dominated by other nations and cultures, struggling to survive without being wholly annihilated. In this context their nature developed a melancholic view of the world, questioning every reaction and attitude reflected towards them; to strangers they often appeared initially mistrustful and sceptical. But once all the facts and intentions about the person he was communicating with became known, Jan quickly became acquainted; he was a warm, happy, funny, supportive and caring human being.

Jan could not stand it if anyone working with him was not enthusiastic about the task, was uninterested, flaccid and lazy. He was not a person to sit back and enjoy the fruits of his labour. He thought it was good not to be satisfied. When you were not satisfied you were urged to carry on, to keep thinking, designing, achieving more. Jan was an immensely talented man and propagating beauty and truth in all he did was his aim. He sought to find beauty, to define it, to create it and

Adolf Loos and Karel Lhota, Villa Müller, Prague, Czech Republic, 1928–30
Villa Müller was Jan Kaplický's favourite Prague building. He visited it as a child, married Eliška Fuchsová there, and his funeral took place there.

give it to the world. He proclaimed that everything was designed, and that the best things were ordinary objects: a coffee cup, a simple drinking glass. A well-designed entity was ageless, it lasted for ever. New, instant ideas poured out of him; what he sketched or modelled would subsequently look like the finished building. He worshipped his architectural heroes: Bertrand Goldberg, Craig Ellwood, Adolf Loos, Oscar Niemeyer and Le Corbusier, and liked reading Ernest Hemingway and Antoine de Saint-Exupéry.

When we met we engaged in gossip about our mutual friends, which Jan loved to hear. If I brought a gift of a Czech mechanical pencil or a good book to read he expressed childlike delight. We exchanged news and planned new writing ventures, but also talked about women and the aesthetic of the female body; its curves and sweeping lines hugely inspired his work. Jan designed daring ladies' dresses, which revealed glimpses of female anatomy. He believed in Adolf Loos' dictum (in his article 'Ladies' Fashion' of 1898): 'Woman clothed herself, and

thus made herself a mystery to man, in order to fill his heart with a longing to solve the mystery.' Jan's new wife Eliška was his vision of the perfect woman.

Jan worried that the worse that could happen after his passing would be that his efforts for better architecture and design would be forgotten and lost. He wanted to be remembered at least for a spoon or a pepper pot he had created. Jan had 10 maxims around which his life and work were moulded: freedom, creativity, people, beauty, elegance, plasticity, sensuality, colour, innovation, inspiration. The best way we can honour Jan's work is to follow in our endeavours and life with at least one of his canons engraved on our hearts. △+

Ivan Margolius is the author and editor of a number of articles and books on architecture and design including *Cubism in Architecture and the Applied Arts* (1979), *Tatra: The Legacy of Hans Ledwinka* (1990), *Skoda Laurin & Klement* (1992), *Prague: A Guide to Twentieth Century Architecture* (1994, 1996), *Jože Plečnik: Church of the Sacred Heart* (1995), *Automobiles by Architects* (2000), *Architects + Engineers = Structures* (2002), the *Architectural Design* issue on *Art + Architecture* (May 2003), *Czech Inspiration* (written with Jan Kaplický, 2005) and *Reflections of Prague: Journeys Through the 20th Century* (2006).

Alice Tully Hall, New York

This sensuous redesign of a 40-year-old concert hall at the Julliard School is the first major project completed by Diller Scofidio + Renfro in their planned remodelling of the entire Lincoln Center for the Performing Arts in New York. Jayne Merkel believes this lively, elegant, personal and welcoming building bodes well for the dozen other public places and performance spaces that the architects will be renovating there over the next few years. It also suggests that the most respectful way to treat historic structures may be to meet them head-on.

At a time when even the most beloved mid-century modern buildings are being threatened with demolition or being garishly remodelled, the once much-maligned 6.5-hectare (16-acre) Lincoln Center campus on the Upper West Side of Manhattan is being imaginatively renovated with sensitivity and style. In 2002, Diller + Scofidio (as the firm was known at the time) won the $1.2 billion commission to restore the entire complex, which contains facilities for the Metropolitan Opera, New York Philharmonic, New York City Opera, New York City Ballet, Film Society of Lincoln Center, School of American Ballet, Julliard School and other institutions.

Lincoln Center was founded in 1956 by a powerful group of New York City business and political leaders to take advantage of available government 'urban renewal' money and create new homes for the Metropolitan Opera and Philharmonic Hall. The planning tsar Robert Moses lent his support, John D Rockefeller III became the president of the fledgling non-profit institution, and the most prominent architects in the US were commissioned to design the buildings: Philip Johnson (the New York State Theater), Wallace Harrison (the Metropolitan Opera House), his partner Max Abramovitz (Philharmonic Hall), Eero Saarinen (the Vivian Beaumont Repertory Theater), Gordon Bunshaft (the New York Public Library for the Performing Arts) and Pietro Belluschi (the Julliard School). Dan Kiley was awarded the landscaping.

Still, the place disappointed. The Philharmonic Hall's much touted modern acoustics turned out to be disastrous; its interior has been rebuilt three times in attempts to improve the sound. The

Diller Scofidio + Renfro with FXFowle, Alice Tully Hall and the Julliard School lobby, 2009
The limestone café bar in front of a new reddish wood-panelled wall terminates in an elegant sharp angle on the south side of the Julliard School lobby, leading to the entrance to Alice Tully Hall on a lower level. The mezzanine-level glass-walled Donors Lounge overlooks the public activity below. The sumptuous and unusual lobby interior is intended to draw people in from the street.

Opera House was garish, and patrons tripped on the shallow plaza steps of the Center. *Time* architecture critic Robert Hughes called the stripped neoclassical design of the complex 'authoritarian'. Few of the 7,000 people whose tenements were destroyed to build the art centre found better housing. And the scheme isolated the concert halls in a marble-clad precinct that contrasted jarringly with the surrounding cityscape.

But the institutions thrived. People flocked to the halls, and new apartment towers (for the well-off), shops and restaurants grew up all around them, energising nearby streets, inflating property values and connecting the largely residential Upper West Side of Manhattan to the midtown business and theatre districts. But Lincoln Center itself still remained an island, deserted when planned events were not taking place, and half a century later all the facilities badly needed updating.

Alice Tully Hall, the main performance space at the Julliard School, is the first to reopen after a $159-million renovation. If Diller Scofidio + Renfro can do as well with the rest of the campus, Lincoln Center will one day be the sensation it was originally intended to be. Clearly the collaboration with the large, experienced New York firm FXFowle, who designed the Condé Nast and Reuters Towers in Times Square, and worked with Renzo Piano on the *New York Times* headquarters, was a success. That practice's Sylvia Smith was willing to help Diller Scofidio + Renfro speak in their own unique language, construction went smoothly and the quality seems very high.

Diller Scofidio + Renfro with FXFowle, The Julliard School, Lincoln Center, New York, 2009

top left: On the Broadway facade, a new glass outer wall encloses 4,180 square metres (45,000 square feet) of new facilities for jazz, dance, rehearsals and recording, which are tucked in over, under or behind the welcoming lobby that faces the street.

top right: An aggressive angled wall now cuts across the corner of Broadway and 65th Street, enlivening the streetscape and enclosing once unused open space to create a more welcoming entrance to the Julliard School, as well as new meeting places and a lively lobby for Alice Tully Hall. The old travertine-clad overhang has been extended all the way to Broadway, where a new glass outer wall invites the public inside.

Pietro Belluschi with Helge Westermann and Eduardo Catalano, The Julliard School, 1969

centre left: The original entrance to Alice Tully Hall was tucked under a gigantic canopy that was sheathed in travertine to relate to other Lincoln Center buildings. Since it was aligned with those buildings and the city grid instead of with the diagonal of Broadway, the sidewalk was therefore unusually wide, darkened by the overhangs, and lifeless. A bridge across 65th Street, closer to the corner than the new one will be when it is constructed mid-block later next year, obstructed ground-level connections with the main Lincoln Center Plaza on the next block.

Diller Scofidio + Renfro with FXFowle and Beyer Blinder Belle, Lincoln Center Plaza and the Julliard School, 2009–10

above: The redesign of the main plaza of the Lincoln Center for the Performing Arts where the Philharmonic Hall (centre), the New York State Theater (left) and the Metropolitan Opera House (not shown) are located involves the extension of the plaza into Columbus Avenue. A street-level drop-off lane is being submerged so that the plaza steps can be extended to the sidewalk. The Julliard School (right), across 65th Street, is now aligned with the complex that its new lobby overlooks. A pedestrian bridge across 65th Street has been moved westward to clear the important corner and better connect with Eero Saarinen's Vivian Beaumont Repertory Theater (behind the Philharmonic Hall and not shown).

This is most apparent inside the hall itself, which was built mainly for chamber music and recitals but is also used for movies, dance and plays. Originally panelled in mahogany, it had a warm feel, but was not elegantly detailed and was difficult to adapt to various purposes. Because there was no smoke exhaust system, scenery violated fire codes. However, the new hall has state-of-the-art equipment of all kinds. Where it took six men six hours to install a screen for film showings, this now takes just three minutes. The four wood-veneered ceiling fly panels, sliding doors behind the stage and eight floor-to-ceiling side-wall panels can swivel around to turn black. And though the continental seating (without a centre aisle) that was popular in the 1960s has been preserved, since generous spacing between rows makes for easy access, the seats themselves have been replaced and covered in grey suede. Even the stage is now automated and can easily be extended in two increments to accommodate audiences ranging from 928 to 1,087.

But the *pièce de résistance* is the new wood-veneer lining. Similar to that which Diller + Scofidio used at the Brasserie Restaurant in the Seagram Building 10 years ago, here it is softer, subtler and all-encompassing, wrapping the interior in African moabi, all from one log, making its surfaces as contiguous as possible. In some areas, a paper-thin layer of the wood is affixed to a thin layer of resin under which is energy-efficient white LED backlighting. When the house lights are turned off, these go on, and the walls seem to glow from within.

To eliminate any unnecessary 'visual noise', the stage has been refitted with a new double-curved edge that makes it melt into the whole. A series of once-separate boxes is now housed in an elongated eye-shaped form on each side wall. Indeed, the entire interior is so cocoon-like that it is almost hard to appreciate the subtlety of the design.

Diller Scofidio + Renfro with FXFowle, Alice Tully Hall and the Julliard School lobby, Lincoln Center, New York, 2009
below left: The Broadway entrance to the Julliard building beckons concert-goers and the general public to enjoy a drink in the lobby of the school and Alice Tully Hall.
below right: The south end of the Julliard School lobby leading to Alice Tully Hall has been elevated, connected to the entrance at Broadway and 65th Street, and sheathed in glass so that theatre-goers can look out at other parts of the Lincoln Center during intermissions. The Philharmonic Hall is visible on the right.

Pietro Belluschi with Helge Westermann and Eduardo Catalano, Alice Tully Hall, 1969
bottom right: The original lower-level lobby of Alice Tully Hall was long, narrow and almost hidden below ground. The steps at the rear, on the east side, led up to the Broadway entrance to the Julliard School.

Diller Scofidio + Renfro with FXFowle, Alice Tully Hall, 2009
above: An almost seamless lining of gold-toned African moabi wood sheathes the walls, stage and ceiling of the redesigned – and substantially simplified – hall. New technological improvements are invisible. But the hall comes to life when the house lights go down and LED lights under the paper-thin veneer give the walls an almost imperceptible glow.

Pietro Belluschi with Helge Westermann and Eduardo Catalano, Alice Tully Hall, 1969
inset: The original hall was mahogany panelled but not particularly subtle. It was intended mainly for chamber music and recitals, but was also used for films, dance and theatre, though it was never quite right for any of them or easy to convert. It also lacked the intimacy that music critics believe enhances acoustics.

This seamlessness creates a greater sense of intimacy with the orchestra, which makes the music sound better, though there has also been a complete (invisible) acoustical upgrade (by JaffeeHolder), which music critics have praised. Even noise from the nearby subway has been muffled by welding tracks and installing rubber pads to absorb the vibrations.

If the interior of the hall is subtle, cosy and comforting, the lobby and street presence is anything but. Here the idea was to create excitement, a sense of place, and to connect the once isolated Lincoln Center campus to the urban fabric. The Julliard School building, where Alice Tully Hall is located, used to be set back from the street with a heavy travertine-clad concrete overhang which sheltered a dark 67-metre (220-foot) long 'plaza' and an entrance that, tucked deep inside, was hard to find. Now the building has been extended out on to Broadway where the facade is sheathed in a glass wall that houses spectacular new first-floor dance studios and a lobby almost 10 times as large. The transparent sheer-glass wall incorporates part of the sidewalk and creates a daring-looking trapezoidal entrance to Julliard on the corner

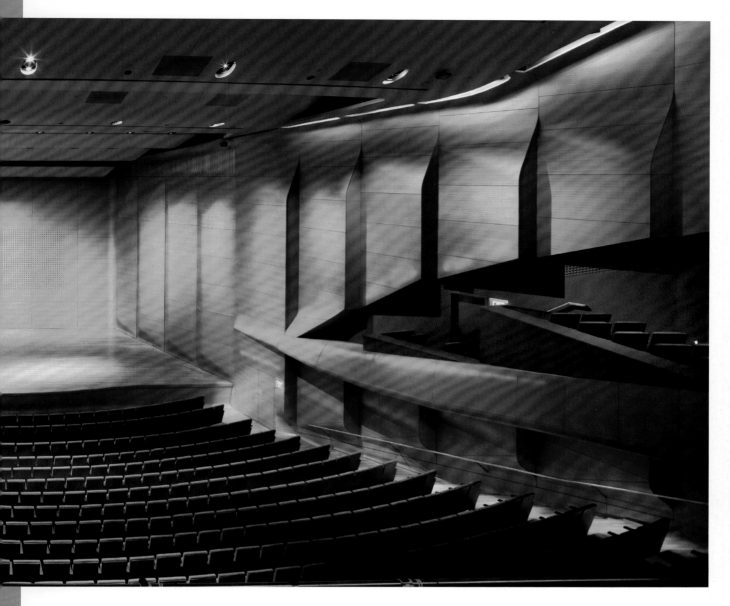

of 65th Street, where Broadway intersects the New York City street grid at a diagonal. It contains some of the largest pieces of glass available, some almost 5 metres (16 feet) high, with the minimum amount of structure possible using tensioned cable rods designed by Arup.

There is another entrance at 66th Street, which is on higher ground. Here the architects used the change in grade to create a long, curved café bar that is level with the ground there but at waist height on the lower level several steps down. The Portuguese limestone bar soars along a curved wall, which is sheathed in vertical strips of Brazilian muirapiranga wood until, at the end of the space, it dissolves in a point like the wing of an aeroplane, leading to the lower-level entrance to Alice Tully Hall.

On the south side, where concert-goers descend some steps to enter the hall, a dramatic glass-walled Donors Lounge, hung by thin rods, overhangs the south side of the Julliard School lobby. On the street level, where 836 square metres (9,000 square feet) of interior space were added, 14 different wall systems now surround the building, providing views of the rest of the Lincoln Center campus across 65th Street where the sidewalk was widened, the street was narrowed, and an aerial bridge was moved further west of Broadway. The architects used changes in ground levels to tuck in rehearsal spaces with clerestory windows. The once-subterranean entrance to Alice Tully Hall now flows off the lively lobby, where there will be a bar, café, restaurant and LED kiosks announcing all the events taking place at Lincoln Center.

'As New Yorkers, it was very selfish,' says Liz Diller. 'We wanted to create a place where we would want to hang out.' Δ+

Text © 2009 John Wiley & Sons Ltd. Images: pp 108-9, 110(tr), 111(l&tr), 112-13 © Iwan Baan; p 110(tl) © David Sundberg/ESTO/VIEW; p 110(cl) © Photo courtesy of the Lincoln Center for Performing Arts, photo Sandor Acs; p 110(b) © Diller Scofidio + Refro; p 111(br) © Photo courtesy of the Lincoln Center for Performing Arts, photo David Lamb; p 112 (inset) © Photo courtesy of the Lincoln Center for Performing Arts, photo Mark Bussell

The Feildbarn

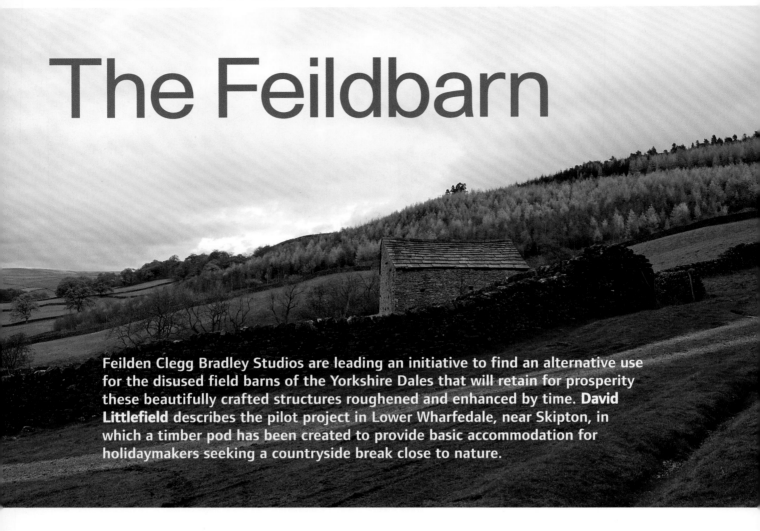

Feilden Clegg Bradley Studios are leading an initiative to find an alternative use for the disused field barns of the Yorkshire Dales that will retain for prosperity these beautifully crafted structures roughened and enhanced by time. David Littlefield describes the pilot project in Lower Wharfedale, near Skipton, in which a timber pod has been created to provide basic accommodation for holidaymakers seeking a countryside break close to nature.

Scattered across the Yorkshire Dales – the rural, rugged and rolling stretch of upland northern England – are more than 4,000 stone barns, one to a field. As farms passed down the generations they became ever more fragmented through subdivision, leaving individual fields cut off from roads and common facilities. The Dales became a patchwork of drystone walls, offering monumentally heavy boundaries between individual fields which came to be provided with their own barns for the shelter of animals and the storage of hay. By the 1960s, however, the needs of farmers and agricultural rules and regulations were changing. The move was towards larger farms and centralised buildings with more generous spatial standards. The field barns began to undergo a slow decline; the value of their agricultural use did not match the cost of their upkeep, and their condition has spiralled downwards ever since. According to the Yorkshire Dales National Park Authority, around 40 per cent of these distinctive little buildings, typically constructed in the 18th and 19th centuries, are in either poor or very poor condition.

To make matters worse, most of them are isolated and unconnected to water and power supplies. Most are very definitely on the small side, and local planning authorities are unsympathetic to wholesale residential adaptation, preferring (perhaps naively) to retain them for agricultural use. One would think these quaint, charming and picturesque field barns were beyond salvation. But a team of architects at Feilden Clegg Bradley Studios is developing an idea, part architectural and part economic, which might just break the cycle of decline. Their idea (inevitably dubbed the Feildbarn) involves the construction of an 'inert and frugal' timber pod inside a barn, providing a rudimentary shelter for holidaymakers whose rental fees will cover the cost of restoring the building itself. The pod is all but invisible from the outside, and occupancy is given away only by the presence of a trailer that provides water and power via an 'umbilical cord'; when the barn is unoccupied, the trailer is towed away. Moreover, it is the barn which provides protection from the weather; the pod, therefore, can be relatively cheap, lightweight and easily removed.

It all sounds relatively straightforward. It looks it too. However, this pilot project in Lower Wharfedale is an exercise in restraint and understatement. Designed with half an eye on the principles of the

Society for the Protection of Ancient Buildings (SPAB),
the little timber insertion in this hillside building certainly
adheres to the maxim that architects should 'complement
not parody' elderly structures: 'New work should express
modern needs in a modern language … if an addition
proves essential, it should not be made to out-do or out-
last the original,' says the society. It also insists that
contemporary designers show a decent respect for the
beauty that comes with age, and that 'bulging, bowing,
sagging and leaning' are qualities to be cared for rather
than 'blemishes to be eradicated'. The barn now
undergoing the attentions of Feilden Clegg Bradley
certainly has its blemishes; it is a sturdy hillside mass of
masonry, very definitely assembled without the
assistance of an architect, within which the pod perches
almost politely. Like Antonello da Messina's 15th-
century depiction of *St Jerome in his Study*, the
temporary insertion is more like a piece of architectural
furniture, although with less capacious surroundings
than the saint.

The two-storey pod occupies just one end of the barn, leaving the
shippon end (with its long-degraded cattle stalls) virtually untouched.
Resting on pads, it shrinks away from the walls. It threads itself
through the rafters and other timberwork of the original building; the
pod's primary window is aligned with that of the barn but, as in the
best traditions of lap dancing, there is a strict 'no touching' rule. For
all its clean lines, machine-cut right angles and polycarbonate panels,
the pod is highly deferential; through the power of contrast its clean,
flat surfaces amplify the colours and textures of its host.

This project, paid for by grants and the architects' own research
fund, may be short-lived. Having been awarded planning permission for
just one year, the practice will monitor the performance of the
structure and assess its suitability for public use before determining its
long-term future with the landowner, the Bolton Abbey Estate. Once
the lessons have been learned, it is perfectly plausible that this pod
will come to be dismantled, leaving the barn better off for its having
been there (a nearby drystone wall has been rebuilt and many years'
worth of accreted muck have been cleared from the interior). But apart
from the architectural merits of the structure, the real future of the
project lies in the potential of its business case. If the number of pods

Feilden Clegg Bradley Studios, The Feildbarn, Lower Wharfedale, Yorkshire, UK, 2009
The upper-level sleeping quarters are accessed by ladder only. The new structure is positioned between the timbers of the original barn structure.

Model of the pod. The insertion is custom-designed for this particular barn, and sits within it like a piece of architectural furniture.

Original timbers, of indeterminate age, are left as reminders of the building's agricultural use. The new cantilevered platform, on which the ladder rests, can be seen in the background.

Antonello da Messina, _Saint Jerome in his Study_, c 1475. Oil on panel, 45.7 x 36.2 cm; National Gallery, London
Like the structure depicted in Antonello da Messina's image of _Saint Jerome in his Study_, painted around 1475, Feilden Clegg Bradley's work fits into the field barn like a piece of architectural furniture. The materiality and architectural languages of insert and 'host' are different, and one can imagine the insertion being removed without any damage to the building itself.

Composite image showing what a larger, family-sized pod might look like (left), and the pod as built (right).

is to expand, they need to be cheap and simple to erect to make them worthwhile for landowners; and although the pilot already seems highly promising in both these respects, farmers need to be persuaded of the merits of conservation and diversifying into the tourist market.

Although it is no easy task, Feilden Clegg Bradley certainly presents a compelling case through the simplicity and integrity of the project, but this begs a question of its own. Just how simple should the pod be? The pilot structure is deliberately low tech: a modest kitchen unit is concealed behind ground-floor cupboard doors, while reaching the first-storey bedroom (insulated with sheep's wool) requires climbing a hefty ladder. Although equipped with a WC and shower, the pod is decidedly basic, offering an exciting alternative to the comforts of bed-and-breakfast accommodation and the back-to-nature frisson of camping. Plans are afoot to develop the concept for family living; when the design

team presented the project to an invited group of architects and engineers, a member of the audience suggested the pod lacked the luxuries and 'bling' expected by today's weekenders. Surely, though, that is the point of this exercise? Feilden Clegg Bradley is attempting to rescue these field barns and celebrate them for what they are. A root and branch transformation is hardly the spirit of the thing. The pod has all the attributes (and romance) of a hayloft, and one can only hope the architects resist the temptation to gild what should remain ungilded. △+

David Littlefield is an architectural writer. He has written and edited a number of books, including *Architectural Voices: Listening to Old Buildings*, published by John Wiley & Sons (October 2007). He was also the curator of the exhibition 'Unseen Hands: 100 Years of Structural Engineering', which ran at the Victoria & Albert Museum in 2008. He has taught at Chelsea College of Art & Design and the University of Bath, and is currently a visiting tutor at the University of the West of England.

Lighting Up

Through the work of London practice Cinimod Studio, led by Dominic Harris, Valentina Croci explores the potential that lighting design offers for interactive work, whether it is transforming unwelcoming urban spaces or enhancing the public's experience of the city.

Cinimod, *Exploded Globe,* **Hoxton Square, London, 2008**
To celebrate the launch of the UK Restaurant and Bar Design Award, Cinimod created a suspended lighting installation that was interactively controlled by visitors from a freestanding plinth located in a corner of the square. Visitors could choreograph the colours of the globe using special punch cards.

Cinimod in collaboration with Peter Coffin, *UFO*, Gdansk, Poland, 2008
This aluminium disk structure measuring 7 metres (23 feet) in diameter was here displayed over 3,000 individually controlled Colour Kinetics LED nodes and suspended by a 50-metre (164-foot) cable attached to an Mi2 helicopter. The UFO lighting effects were remotely controlled by SMS text messages sent by spectators.

Interactive lighting installations in public spaces continue to demonstrate a significant level of technical experimentation and technological content. The vast majority are temporary and related to a specific event, allowing spectators to experience everyday spaces in completely new ways. This is no small feat as it offers designers new parameters of investigation that are part of a progressively more interdisciplinary approach to design.

One of the groups operating in this field is young London office Cinimod Studio. Specialists in interactive lighting design, Cinimod was founded in 2007 by Dominic Harris who had previously collaborated with Jason Bruges, Softroom Architects and Future Systems. His company recently illuminated Hoxton Square in London with a 3-metre (9.8-foot) globe, and floated a flying disc over the skies of Gdansk in Poland (the latter project was realised in collaboration with the New York artist Peter Coffin). Both lighting installations (*Exploded Globe* and *UFO*) include active participation of the public. Using different instruments – punch cards in the first project and SMS text messages in the second – spectators are able to modify the lighting effects produced by the installation. 'One of the final objectives of this type of intervention is that of allowing individuals a more active control of public space,' says Harris. 'The urban context or architecture itself must be part of the user's experience in order to assume meaning. Above all in public space,

this type of interactive installation allows us to transmit new contents and forms of narration to urban space and define a new relationship with the architecture of the past.'

Interactive works in public spaces function as a topological medium: they allow the user to create a personal memory and experience tied to place. Harris continues: '*Exploded Globe* in Hoxton Square was used to transform a less than welcoming space. The object played an active role by introducing a soft and shifting light that rendered the square a more pleasurable and safer place; it also played a social role which, by involving the general public, animated the entire square and highlighted a new way of using public space. The reaction of the spectators underlined the need for something permanent, something beneficial to the entire city.'

The duration of an interactive installation is also a crucial factor in its design, defining both the type of project (materials, technologies and content) and the methods of interaction with users. Form, time and technology determine the interactive effects which, in turn, condition the user's experience. What is more, the duration of the installation comports, on the one hand, specific issues of efficiency, safety and maintenance and, on the other, the much more complex overlapping of the content of the work with the movement of its users. In fact, in the case of a permanent installation, the everyday activity of the user is joined with the performance of the installation, with possible problems of redundancy or the weakening of its meaning. 'Designers, architects and artists are responsible for designing works that maintain a relationship with the user over time. As a result, for me it is important that the content and the visual effects are connected with the physical context and what takes place around the installation, such as, for example, the movement and actions of passers-by. I do not believe in the projection of messages or predefined lighting effects,' says Harris. At present interactive installations in public spaces are temporary, and have precise objectives. 'We are still in a phase of experimentation, however these examples of "event architecture" or "event artwork" serve as tests for the development of prototypes and technological applications to be applied to buildings or in public spaces in a permanent manner.'

Works that create an immediate relationship with the actions of the user include Cinimod's *Beacon* (an installation at the Dublin Science Gallery and Kinetica Art Fair in February and March 2009), in which a series of beacon lamps, normally used by the police in emergencies, are fitted with electronic apparatus that controls the intensity and direction of the beams of light. External video cameras follow the movement and position of spectators, allowing the lamps to track the movement of visitors who cross the path of the installation. When

there is more than one person in the space, the movement of the lights becomes playful and unexpected. 'What I like about the project is its immediacy: independent of the age and experience of users, anyone can interact with the piece, without the need for further explanation. This is very stimulating in terms of design,' says Harris.

Interactive installations in public facilities, such as restaurants or bars, can change the user's perception of the quality of a particular environment. Cinimod has recently completed an installation in South Kensington, London, for the first in a series of shops in the UK being opened by the Korean chain Snog, which sells frozen yoghurt. The shop is characterised by a fresh aesthetic and a digital ceiling-sky, the projected atmospheric effects of which change according to exterior climatic conditions: if it is hot outside, the store's ceiling features cool, refreshing images; when cold, a warm summer sun, for example, is projected. 'It is a simple example that demonstrates how, even in such a small and confined area, it is possible to alter the quality of space,' says Harris. 'Client reaction has been very positive: the public feels immediately at home and involved.'

This type of site-specific operation has allowed Cinimod to develop a series of products that capitalise on technological experimentation – for example, the use of LEDs and systems of digital control – to create

Cinimod in collaboration with Chris O'Shea,
***Beacon*, Dublin Science Gallery, Ireland, and Kinetica Art Fair, London, February and March 2009**
An array of emergency beacon lights interacts with visitors, tracking their movement through the space in real time and creating an immersive and playful experience.

Cinimod, Snog Restaurant, Soho, London, 2009
This is the first of a chain of new restaurants to be opened in the UK. The fresh aesthetic of the shop creates the feeling of a never-ending summer. The ceiling, comprising 700 glass globes of controlled light, is the main attraction and creates a bubble-effect glow.

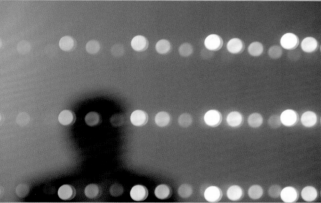

Cinimod, *Interactive Tableaux* prototype, 2008
The panels, a limited edition of three pieces, are comprised of a highly engineered build-up of four different glass types, LEDs, embedded electronic control and aluminium. The objects are engaging, creating colour and virtual shadows in reaction to the movements of passers-by.

interactive furnishings for the domestic environment and private spaces. This is the case with their *October Table* and *Interactive Tableaux*, two mirrored objects to be used in domestic spaces, whose interior lamps are activated by the movement of users in proximity to the objects.

With regard to the future of interactive digital lighting installations, Harris says: 'We are moving towards their use in larger structures, such as buildings, as architects are asking themselves how they can take advantage of the potentials offered by this field. In analogous terms, these types of works are destined to become more frequent in public spaces. I am working with landscape designers, with whom I am examining the transformation of the profession of lighting design and landscape architecture. Due to new advanced technologies and the range of available products, traditional lighting fixtures and the rules for designing in public space no longer make sense. We are also working towards reinventing public gardening and developing new outdoor products with interactive characteristics that transform the way we perceive and use the city.' 𝚫+

Translated from the Italian version into English by Paul David Blackmore.

Valentina Croci is a freelance journalist of industrial design and architecture. She graduated from Venice University of Architecture (IUAV), and attained an MSc in architectural history from the Bartlett School of Architecture, London. She achieved a PhD in industrial design sciences at the IUAV with a theoretical thesis on wearable digital technologies.

Seawater Greenhouses and the Sahara Forest Project

In this issue, Ken Yeang joins forces with Michael Pawlyn of Exploration Architecture Ltd to investigate how seawater, when combined with the biological know-how of a beetle, might hold the key for creating fresh water in desert environments.

Water is a precondition of life, and the lack of water in many parts of the world is the root cause of much suffering and poverty. Present methods of supply in arid regions such as the Middle East include extraction from ground reserves, the diversion of water from other regions and, in most instances, via desalination, which is energy intensive. However, none of these methods is sustainable in the long term. Inequitable distribution inevitably leads to conflict.

We are all aware of our dependence on water, but perhaps not always cognisant of just how critically dependent we truly are. For example, to make a kilogram of coffee requires 20,000 litres (4,398 gallons) of water. For a quarter-pound hamburger, the water required is 11,000 litres (2,419 gallons). For a simple cotton T-shirt, the water required is 7,000 litres (1,539 gallons).

Ecologists contend that it was the colonisation of the land by plants that was primarily responsible for creating the moderate climate that has prevailed in recent geological times. The converse is also true: the loss of vegetation exacerbates climate change. Since the dawn of civilisation, forests have been shrinking and deserts have been growing, primarily as a consequence of our human activity – a trend that continues to this day. We need to find ways to reverse desertification and, through this process, to mitigate climate change.

Taking inspiration from a beetle that harvests its own water in a desert, the Sahara Forest Project (a collaboration between Exploration Architecture Ltd, Seawater Greenhouse Ltd and Max Fordham LLP) is an innovative and synergistic combination of two proven technologies that produces fresh water from seawater as well as producing food and energy in a zero-carbon way.

One major element of the scheme is the Seawater Greenhouse which essentially mimics the biosphere's hydrological cycle in miniature. The system creates a cool growing environment in hot, arid parts of the world and is a net producer of distilled water from seawater. Seawater is evaporated from cardboard grilles at the front of the greenhouse to create cool humid air which is then condensed as distilled water at the back. Various versions of the scheme (designed by Charlie Paton of Seawater Greenhouse Ltd) have been built in Tenerife, Oman and the United Arab Emirates.

The second element of the system is concentrated solar power (CSP). This uses an array of solar-tracking mirrors to concentrate the heat of the sun to create steam that drives conventional turbines, producing zero-carbon electricity twice as efficiently as photovoltaic technology.

The synergy of the Seawater Greenhouse and CSP systems makes the economic case even more attractive. Both work extremely well in hot desert conditions. While the former produces large quantities of surplus heat, the latter makes use of this to evaporate seawater. The Seawater Greenhouse system produces large quantities of pure deionised water that the CSP plants, in return, need for their turbines and for cleaning the CSP system's mirrors to maintain maximum efficiency.

The combined system is now being proposed as a large-scale component of an urban infrastructure to produce fresh water from seawater, as well as renewable electrical energy and food. The electrical energy generated would be distributed to local users or, via a direct current (DC) connection, to other parts of the region with minimal energy loss.

The Seawater Greenhouse by itself is self-sufficient in fresh water – evaporating approximately 50 cubic metres (1,766 cubic feet) of seawater and harvesting 5 cubic metres (176 cubic feet) of fresh water per hectare (2.471 acres) per day. The addition of CSP and a low-humidity location could further increase the water production by several times, thereby generating a surplus of fresh water.

Exploration Architecture, Seawater Greenhouse and Max Fordham LLP, Sahara Forest Project, 2008–

above: The Sahara Forest Project is a combination of two proven technologies: the Seawater Greenhouse and concentrated solar power (CSP). *left*: The Namibian fog-basking beetle has evolved a way to harvest water from the air in a desert environment. It emerges at night and, by radiating heat to the night sky, becomes slightly cooler than its surroundings. When the moist breeze blows in off the sea, droplets of water form on the beetle's shell. The water is then funnelled down to the beetle's mouth. The Seawater Greenhouse is similar in the way that it creates condensing surfaces and supplies these with humidified air.

This surplus of fresh water could make other activities, besides human consumption, possible, such as the production of Jatropha, an energy crop that can be grown in soils with low levels of nutrient that would not support food crops. The resulting biofuel production from the crop could be used to fuel transportation and to maintain base-load energy generation at night.

A guiding principle on the project has been to consider anything that is under-utilised as an opportunity for adding elements to the system to achieve greater resource efficiency. The Seawater Greenhouse system only recondenses about a tenth of the seawater that it evaporates. The rest is lost out of the back as humid air. One way in which this could be transformed into an opportunity is to find a location with higher terrain downwind so that the humid air would be forced to rise and form a mist. Fog nets can then be used to capture the moisture and funnel it down to tree saplings (an approach pioneered on Lanzarote by Dr Robert Schemenauer), which could allow the revegetation of areas of desert land.

This composite system shows how combining two proven technologies in a new way can produce multiple benefits: producing fresh water from seawater, large amounts of renewable energy and food, as well as reversing desertification. The scheme is an example of biomimicry – an approach to design and invention that derives inspiration from natural organisms for survival in resource-constrained environments. Ecosystems, for example, are also models of closed-loop resource use in which there are beneficial symbiotic relationships where the waste from one organism becomes the nutrient for another.

The Sahara Forest Project could be realised as part of a sustainable component for ecocities, providing the necessary eco-infrastructural requirements in a zero-carbon way. *D+*

Michael Pawlyn is the director of Exploration Architecture Ltd and is collaborating on the Sahara Forest Project with Seawater Greenhouse Ltd and Max Fordham LLP. He previously worked with Grimshaw Architects (1997–2007) and was instrumental in the design development of the Eden Project in Cornwall.

Ken Yeang is a director of Llewelyn Davies Yeang in London and TR Hamzah & Yeang, its sister company, in Kuala Lumpur, Malaysia. He is the author of many articles and books on sustainable design, including *Ecodesign: A Manual for Ecological Design* (Wiley-Academy, 2006).

Parallel Indexing
Infrastructure and Space

As governments around the world open the public coffers in an attempt to pull their economies back from collapse, **Holger Kehne and Jeff Turko** describe how they have extended the work of the Architectural Association Diploma Unit 12 to incorporate the pertinent subject of infrastructure and architecture, employing 'indexical systems'.

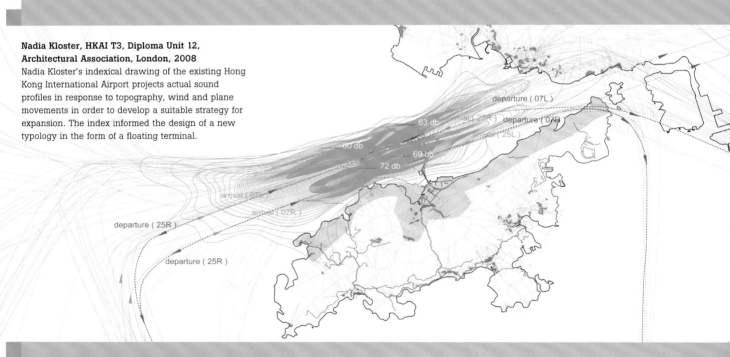

Nadia Kloster, HKAI T3, Diploma Unit 12, Architectural Association, London, 2008
Nadia Kloster's indexical drawing of the existing Hong Kong International Airport projects actual sound profiles in response to topography, wind and plane movements in order to develop a suitable strategy for expansion. The index informed the design of a new typology in the form of a floating terminal.

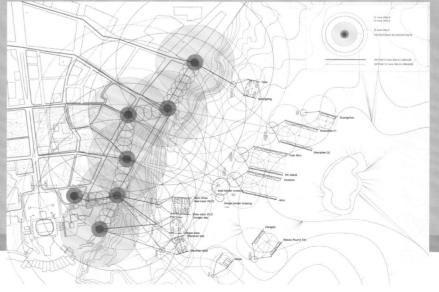

Julia Li, Xhuhai Ferry Terminal and Coastal Park, Diploma Unit 12, Architectural Association, London, 2008
Julia Li's indexical drawing of Xhuhai's waterfront in China renders the core relationships between the existing urban layout, with regard to walking distance and the bay's topography and tidal movement with a view towards projecting a new ferry terminal that adapts to both. The index and proposal led to integrated transport hubs and public spaces positioned strategically to provide vitality for the waterfront.

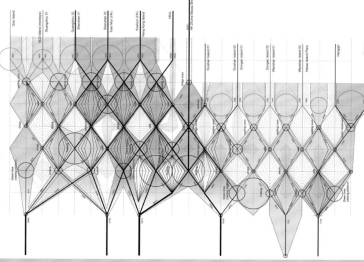

Nadia Kloster, HKAI T3, Diploma Unit 12,
Architectural Association, London, 2008
The rendering of Nadia Kloster's final new
terminal design highlights the accessible
roofscape from where the physical
surrounding waterscape can be appreciated.

Julia Li, Xhuhai Ferry Terminal and Coastal Park,
Diploma Unit 12, Architectural Association, London, 2008
Julia Li developed a diagram in the form of an abstract matrix able to negotiate
the intertwining of land and water in relation to a network of pedestrian paths.
Developed from the initial index, this enabled her design to synthesise
infrastructure, topography and experience in a single holistic system.

The last two decades of market-led, neoliberal structural
development with its resistance to public spending has
seriously endangered the future performance of
infrastructure, while also diminishing the quantity, quality
and role of public space. Architecture has been stripped
of its ambitions as a social entity. Even public buildings
are now procured, organised and run as private entities,
while having to absorb some of the needs of public
identity through an often exaggerated iconography.

Credit crunch-induced, socioeconomic policy revisions
offer the opportunity to question these developments and
reinvigorate the public role within the production of
space. Many billions of public spending is going to be
allocated to infrastructural projects. Ideally, this money
would go not just on the repair of existing bridges or be
allocated to building new transportation links, but also on
architecture and public space as part of the equation.

The Architectural Association (AA) Diploma Unit 12
proposes exploiting potential synergies through a
concurrent engagement of infrastructure and architecture,
and has set out to develop a series of concepts and tool-
sets to address these issues. It is now expanding on such
design methodologies through the engagement of
qualitative means in order to evaluate, reach out to and
communicate the vision and experience of such an
integrated urbanism.

Indexical and Sensitive Systems
Holger Kehne and Eva Castro kicked off Diploma Unit 12
in 2003–04 with a programme that focused on the slopes
of Venezuela's coastline, which had been devastated by

landslides the previous year. This was the start of a
continuous preoccupation with man-made landscape and
infrastructure as space, and subsequent years dealt with
extreme environmental and infrastructural conditions in
Mexico City (2004–05) and Dubai (2006–07), as well as
the impact of rapid development on transportation nodes
in the Pearl River Delta (2007–08).

In dealing with such issues, the unit continues to be
concerned with the development of an 'architectural
indexicality'. Examples for an index are a thermometer
indexing temperature or a weathervane that indexes the
direction of the wind.[1]

In Diploma Unit 12, students produce indexical
drawings and models through translating environmental,
structural, organisational and morphological conditions
into gradient fields of varying intensity. Their immediate
spatial value may literally form the basis for a subsequent
design proposal. In other cases they become
instrumental in fostering, strategising and evaluating the
design process.

At a second stage these fields become interpreted and
parametrically organised to form 'sensitive systems':
working methodologies that enable students to grow new
organisations from within existing systems. Their scale,
distribution, organisation and potential become integrated
through the formation of a proto-morphological matrix
that helps to guide the subsequent design process
towards cohesion and reverberance between existing and
new. At the same time the scope for interpretation,
evaluation and choice is unlimited, as is the potential for
radically new interpretations and consequences.

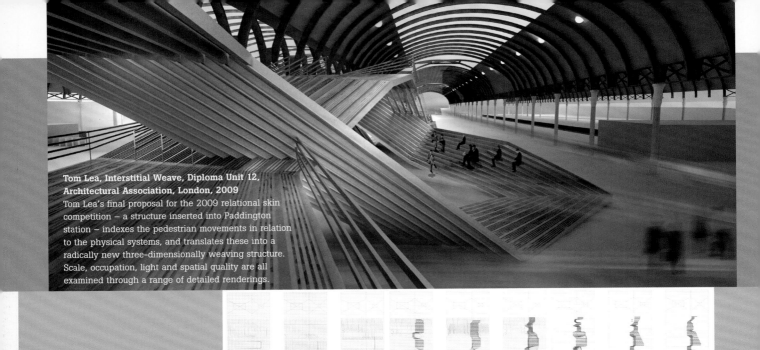

Tom Lea, Interstitial Weave, Diploma Unit 12,
Architectural Association, London, 2009
Tom Lea's final proposal for the 2009 relational skin
competition – a structure inserted into Paddington
station – indexes the pedestrian movements in relation
to the physical systems, and translates these into a
radically new three-dimensionally weaving structure.
Scale, occupation, light and spatial quality are all
examined through a range of detailed renderings.

Post-Indexical and Assertive Figures

*There is a new generic subject who, inundated by
media, information, and images, has less motivation
for other, more interpretive kinds of information. It
is not that the subject cannot understand or closely
read an architectural object; rather it is that the
subject does not have the means to bridge the gap
between the discipline of architecture as it was
known in the past and in its present incarnations.*
        Peter Eisenman, 'The Post-Indexical: A Critical
                                            Option', 2008[2]

Diploma Unit 12's scope developed in the last two years
aligned with Eisenman's observations to produce post-
indexical conditions: projects that are based on the
indexicality of environmental, social and spatial registers
yet communicate their specificity without the need to
refer them back to this. Existing tools were mended and
additional ones sought in order to foster a shift from the
adaptive and integrated towards open-ended assertive
design strategies.

The first of these is the diagram, which though regularly
employed previously now becomes central to the design
process. The diagram as used by the unit should not be
confused with an abstract version of the design proposal or
some specific way of representing aspects of it; it is used
for its projective potential as described by Deleuze: 'The
diagrammatic or abstract machine does not function to
represent, even something real, but rather constructs a
real that is yet to come, a new type of reality.'[3]

The diagram thus has the potential to engage local forces
and conditions directly and before the implementation of
material and technology. [4]

The second new mode of engagement is with iconography itself.
While the intention remains to expand and diffuse architecture's
boundaries, including visual ones, it cannot be ignored that, in power
and instrumentality, the image in many aspects exceeds the scope of
the physical. It also provides an opportunity to focus on the actual
experience of space itself, its quality and character. In this manner the
unit is incorporating visualisation into the index with the aim of avoiding
the visual sound-bite, and transforming it into a means of analysing and
evaluating as well as presenting the author's architectural vision.

This year the unit is exploring rail infrastructure. Starting with a
small-scale design competition, students were asked to insert public
space into infrastructure. This took the form of a tangible modulated
skin/envelope for Paddington station, one of London's main multinodal
infrastructural hubs. Creating space that takes advantage of the
obvious and latent potentials within the ubiquitous arrangement of
pedestrian and vehicular flows and added commerce, the new skin
formation interacts with, alters or complements the existing functional
template. The aim here is to elevate the space from its mundane,
problem-solving status to a contemporary civic place where a multitude
of activities, encounters and experiences can take place.

The unit is currently working on developing a high-speed train link
along the length of Chile from the tropics to the sub-Antarctic glaciers.
All along the line, a string of railway stations will engage with radically
different local conditions.

In cross section, the project's territory slopes from the 6,000-metre
(19,685-foot) peaks of the Andes down to the Pacific. Digital tools are
used as means of addressing this topographic variety and articulating
the multiple ground planes and complex 3-D relationships involved.

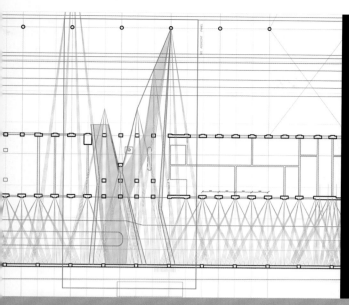

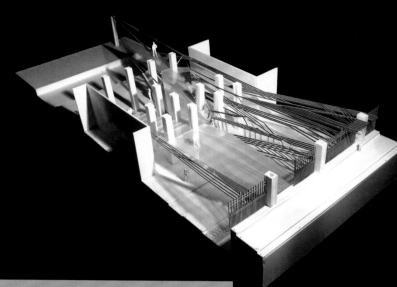

Mark Chan, Oscillating Vectors, Diploma Unit 12, Architectural Association, London, 2009
Mark Chan proposes the replacement of the existing canopy over the departures road at the side of Paddington station with a pair of smaller canopies that index the modular differences between the exterior face of Macmillan House and the iron bars above the retaining wall. Simultaneously sheltering the taxi drop-off area and performing as a bridge that forms a new direct connection between train tracks and bus stops on the main street level, the structure is a direct derivative of the initial index.

Many of the stations will be located in urban environments, traversing the different conditions: tracks and rail buildings will be interwoven with the surrounding city while articulating new spatial configurations. Each student will study one of the projected stations and its corresponding climatic zone, geography, geology, landscape or urban environment. Responding to this climatic diversity, the unit will develop building envelopes and skins that will serve as mechanisms of environmental modulation as well as socially and experientially operative formations.

The Diploma Unit 12 programme highlights the need to develop new, meaningful relationships between local and global scales and conditions. The ambition of such multiscale systems should not be restricted to solving existing problems, and extends to the generation of new possibilities and relationships between the city, its occupants, the landscape and its sociopolitical environment: a structured field condition that deploys architecture as its main nodal articulation. **⌂+**

Notes
1. 'For Charles Peirce, "indexicality" is one of three sign modalities and is a phenomenon far broader than language. Anything we can construe as a sign that points to something – including a weathervane (an index of wind direction), or smoke (an index of fire) – is operating indexically. In the human realm, social indexicality includes any sign (clothing, speech variety, table manners) that points to, and helps create, social identity.'

See Wikipedia: http://en.wikipedia.org/wiki/Indexical.
2. From Peter Eisenman, 'The Post-Indexical: A Critical Option', in Penelope Dean (ed), *Hunch 11: Rethinking Representation*, Episode Publishers (Rotterdam), 2007, pp 18–25.
3. Gilles Deleuze and Félix Guattari, *A Thousand Plateaus*, Athlone Press (London), 2001, p 142.
4. 'Diagrams should not be understood as instrumentalized ideas, as this could be construed as deterministic. Instead, diagrams should be understood as conceptual techniques that come before any particular technology.' Greg Lynn, 'Forms of Expression: The Proto-Functional Potential of Diagrams', in *Folds, Bodies & Blobs: Collected Essays*, La Lettre Volée (Brussels), 1998, pp 223–32.

Holger Kehne is an architect and has been a Diploma Unit 12 Unit Master since 2003. He is a founding partner of Plasma Studio (www.plasmastudio.com) and GroundLab (www.groundlab.org). He has received the Next Generation Architects Award, Young Architect of the Year Award, HotDip Galvanizing Award and the ContractWorld Award. His work has been published widely in international books and journals.

Jeff Turko is the founder of the design practice NEKTON (www.nekton.org), and is also a member of OCEAN (www.ocean-designresearch.net). He studied at the AA School of Architecture where he received the AA Diploma in 1999, and has been a Diploma Unit 12 Unit Master since 2008. He also teaches architecture at the University of East London School of Architecture and Visual Arts.

'Unit Factor' is edited by Michael Weinstock, who is Academic Head and Master of Technical Studies at the Architectural Association School of Architecture in London. He is co-guest-editor with Michael Hensel and Achim Menges of the *Emergence: Morphogenetic Design Strategies* (May 2004) and *Techniques and Technologies in Morphogenetic Design* (March 2006) issues of *Architectural Design*. He is currently writing a book on the architecture of emergence for John Wiley & Sons Ltd.

McLean's Nuggets

Frequency Formworks: Musique Concrète

In 1777 German physicist Christoph Lichtenberg discovered that dust particles formed distinctive figures on positively or negatively charged fields, making electricity and the flow of electricity visible for the first time. Eleven years later another German physicist, Ernst Chladni, discovered that by agitating metal and glass plates covered with a thin dusting of quartz, one could form patterns or what Chladni described as 'sound figures',[1] and by varying the size and thickness of the plates (and thus their resonant frequency) so the intricate patterns change. Chladni thus created an analogue alphabet of sounds and not the more familiar representational notations of frequency – the notes on a musical score. In 1967 Hans Jenny, a Swiss physician and anthroposophist, devised Cymatics[2] (the study of wave phenomena); his experiments, based on Chladni's, extended the excitation of materials into the third dimension. Whereas Chladni had collated a two-dimensional alphabet of signs or figures, Jenny was creating forms in liquids, powders and gels that changed dynamically with the input of audible sine waves and the control of their frequency and amplitude.

If we transpose Jenny's technology to the casting of materials such as concrete, it may indeed be possible to create large-scale highly articulated cast surfaces with 'standing wave'[3] frequencies. This literal excitement of concrete through sound obviates the need for complex formwork, utilising a kind of 'tuned up' steel reinforcement to transmit these good vibrations to create a new fabrication process. Thus, by playing a fixed 'standing wave' tone into a container of liquid concrete until the concrete is set, we may finally be able to deliver Goethe's frozen music and the realised building product of composer Pierre Schaeffer's *musique concrète*.

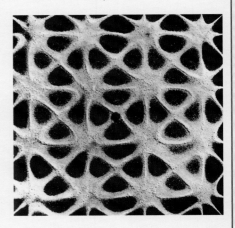

A sonorous figure, produced by a piezoelectric excitation of 6,700 hertz.

Booze Queues

It is difficult to imagine any reasonable justification for the waiting in line that is the queue. Likewise a recent Transport for London competition for the redesign of London's 12,000 bus stops (subsequently scrapped) seemed to encourage a misdirected effort in finessed artefacts, whereas the successful design of a system of transport would surely not include an abundance of waiting around time, unless of course the waiting around time is indeed part of the design. The substantial improvement of a bus service (for example, increased frequency) will obviate any need to form a line with a beginning and an end, because those waiting will be sufficiently confident that there will in fact be space for everyone on board. The study of the queue and queuing is appropriately lengthy, with the classic of the genre a very readable *Queues* by DR Cox and Walter L Smith.[4] Originally published in 1961, it remains a fascinating study in operational research, probability theory and applied mathematics. Congestion in queues is looked at by studying arrival patterns; regular arrival patterns are physically simplest, but hard to compute, whereas random arrival patterns are mathematically the simplest.

One large area of study is how to deter the individual from joining a queue in the first place, which becomes a psychological conundrum when faced with the possibility that a long queue may get even longer ... so I'd better join it.

In a recent report in *The Times* newspaper,[5] one such queue-joining deterrent has been suggested by Scottish parliamentarians. Eager to reduce the ill effects of alcoholic overindulgence, Nationalist ministers have suggested a separate queue for alcohol in supermarkets, which would 'help to emphasise that alcohol is not an ordinary product'. Opposition critics have immediately decried this proto 'walk of shame' as an attack on civil liberties.

Meanwhile, in an interview with the *Daily Telegraph* 'Travel' section,[6] Ryanair chief executive Michael O'Leary explained that the airline intends to remove all of its check-in desks by the end of this year – one less queue and one more opportunity for wily salespersons.

Metamaterials

In the world of material strangeness, an article in *Nano*, 'The magazine for small science', introduces us to a curious class of stuffs called 'metamaterials'. In 1967, Russian physicist Victor Veselago had suggested the possibility of an optical material with a negative refractive index that, as such, could refract (bend) light in the opposite direction making light flow backwards as if reflected in an invisible mirror. This theory suggests that it is possible to create a material that is invisible, or more precisely, a material that might 'cloak' the visibility of other visible materials.

It was Sir John Pendry, while experimenting with radar-absorbing materials for Marconi, who suggested that, as light is only a small sliver of the electromagnetic spectrum, these metamaterials could theoretically operate at a number of different frequencies across the spectrum, extending the idea of the 'invisibility cloak' to areas such as acoustics. Quoted in the *Nano* article, Pendry said: 'We may also be able to make an acoustic cloak, which some people with noisy neighbours might welcome!'[7] So not only might we not see something, we may not hear it either.

Dr David R Smith of Duke University has described metamaterials as left-handed, and states: 'In a left-handed medium, light propagates (or appears to move) in the opposite direction as energy flows.'[8] The first demonstration of a metamaterial with negative refractive index was demonstrated by Dr Smith at the University of California, San Diego, in 2000.

The interest within the nanotechnology community is in building with nano-scaled circuitry, which can locally manipulate the direction of visible light using metamaterials. Pendry said: 'In principle, we can literally make electromagnetic energy go where we please, though practicalities do limit this.'[9]

So the possibilities of metamaterials are not limited to a kind of illusionist's dream, but could be employed at a nano-scale in miniaturised electronics or the 'metactronics'[10] developed by Nader Engheta (University of Pennsylvania), who is developing nanocircuits[11] using visible and infrared frequencies in place of electrons. Δ+

'McLean's Nuggets' is an ongoing technical series inspired by Will McLean and Samantha Hardingham's enthusiasm for back issues of *AD*, as explicitly explored in Hardingham's *AD* issue *The 1970s is Here and Now* (March/April 2005).

Will McLean is joint coordinator of technical studies (with Pete Silver) in the Department of Architecture at the University of Westminster. He recently co-authored, also with Pete Silver, the book *Introduction to Architectural Technology* (Laurence King, 2008).

Notes
1. Theodor W Adorno, 'The Form of the Phonograph Record', *October*, Vol 55, Winter, 1990, pp 56–61. Trans Thomas Y Levin.
2. Hans Jenny, *Cymatics*, MACROmedia Press (Newmarket, New Hampshire), 2001.
3. A standing wave is a static waveform caused by the interference of equal and opposite (in amplitude) reflected waves.
4. David Roxbee Cox and Walter L Smith, *Queues*, Chapman Hall & CRC Press (London), 1961.
5. Angus Macleod, Scottish Political Editor, 'Drinkers to Face "Walk of Shame" at Supermarket Checkouts,' *The Times*, 18 June 2008.
6. See http://www.telegraph.co.uk/travel/travelnews/4732634/Ryanair-to-remove-airport-check-in-desks.html.
7. Elaine Mulcahy, 'A Trick of the Light?', *Nano*, Issue 6, April 2008, pp 16–19.
8. http://physics.ucsd.edu/lhmedia/whatis.html.
9. Mulcahy, op cit.
10. http://www.nanowerk.com/spotlight/spotid=2947.php.
11. Nader Engheta, 'Circuits with Light at Nanoscales: Optical Nanocircuits Inspired by Metamaterials', *Science*, Vol 317, No 5845, 21 September 2007, pp 1698–1702.

Diagram showing light passing though a refractive (a) and negative refractive (b) index medium.

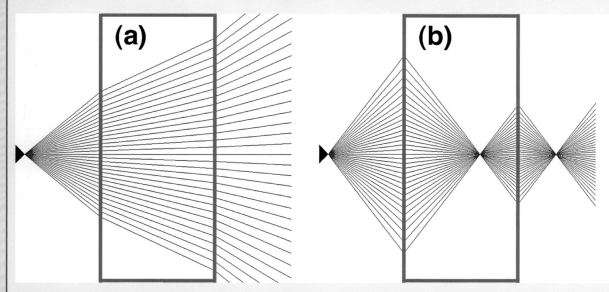

Parallel Biological Futures

Neil Spiller looks beyond the digital and envisions a surreal future of 'biological parallelism' that pushes the boundary of architecture deep into the natural sciences, potentially creating 'huge rafts of new architectural flora and fauna'.

I was asked recently to present a swift series of architectural thoughts at a Design Dinner (guests included some of the best-known architects in London town) at Westminster City Council. My fellow speaker was Peter Cook. In our own ways we both tried to entice the assembled crowd to be more innovative with their architectural visions and the council to be more accommodating of these visions. However, I felt duty-bound to explain a few home truths about architects and current computer technology.

It is important for all those involved in the production of architecture and its theory, discussion and legislation to understand that computers have aided the design of funny-shaped roofs since the late 1960s, the 'evolution'

of form using genetic algorithms since the early 1990s, and building elements that talk to each other since the late 1970s. So we must stop justifying our supposed contemporary architectural visions in relation to these, by now, quite standard techniques. We must also, however, see the near future of architecture and its discourse as being about the relationship between objects and spaces as opposed to the simple creation of iconic form. In this respect, I also do not mean harping on about the blinding drug of parametrics, but something much more profound.

We are not using the full scope of the lexicon that is currently being offered to us. I would like to introduce to you 'parallel architectural biology'. While working with these ideas I have been inspired by Leo Lionni's gorgeous surrealist spoof *Parallel Botany* (1977). The book jacket describes its contents thus:

Eirini Adroutsopoulou, Reflexive Lagoon, MArch(Architectural Design)AVATAR, Bartlett School of Architecture, London, 2006
Located within the canals and lagoon of Venice, the project rejoices in the phenomenology of the area: its tides, silt, gentle decomposition and winds. A series of sensors and drivers constantly sense, quiver and activate subtle architectural conversations making visible the changing dynamics and Venice's fragile equilibrium. High-tech artificial reeds and nests that mix realities, memories and sensations are symbiotically entwined with the natural ecology and biology. This close architectural relationship between the natural and the artificial is becoming more and more focused on the biology of cells. 'Parallel architectural biology' seeks to manipulate the dynamics of cells to architectural advantage.

With precision, with authority, with wit, with ineffable brilliance of supreme scholarship, Leo Lionni, in his book 'Parallel Botany', presents the first full-scale guide to the world of parallel plants – a vast, ramified, extremely peculiar, and wholly imaginary plant kingdom. It is a botany alive with wonders from *Tirillus silvador* of the High Andes (whose habit it is to emit shrill whistles on clear nights in January and February) to the woodland Tweezers (it was a Japanese parallel botanist Uchigaki who first noticed the unsettling relationship between the growth pattern of a group of Tweezers and a winning layout of Go).[1]

As architects we are now starting to have the wherewithal to create great works of 'biological parallelism'. These new works will push the boundaries of architecture deep into botany and biology, and talk of time-based architectural space, ethics and new technology, ecology, different ways of seeing, epistemology, cyborgian geography and archaeology. We can use the natural imperatives of plants and maybe animal cells as a means to 'rewire' them to create huge rafts of new architectural flora and fauna. We might be able to make truly sustainable and green materials whose biodegradability is simply a natural side effect of these technologies. Obviously, the ethics of these technologies must be frequently debated. The application of ethics to architecture is in its infancy, no matter what the old Modernists might say.

As Lionni has observed, these technologies have the ability to be highly surreal (another reason they interest me). Dr Rachel Armstrong and I will be guest-editing an issue of *AD* with the results of our experiments in 'biological parallelism' in due course, but in the meantime it is important to note that some of the Bartlett School of Architecture's more experimental postgraduate students are already taking large steps towards these new synthesised ecologies and biologies.

Perhaps I should leave the last word to Professor Roy Ascott:

Cyberbotany once established and integrated into 21st-century culture, as I believe will eventually be the case, would cover a wide spectrum of activity and Investigation into, on the one hand, the properties and potential of artificial life forms within the cyber and nano ecologies, and, on the other, the technoetic dimensions and psychoactive effects of *banisteriopsis caapi* and other such vegetal products of nature.[2]

A new moist architectural world that is ready to be explored. Watch this space. *AD*+

Notes
1. Leo Lionni, *Parallel Botany*, Alfred A Knopf (New York), 1977.
2. Roy Ascott, 'Beyond Boundaries: Edge-Life: Technoetic Structures and Moist Media', *Art, Technology Consciousness*, intellect (Bristol), 2000, p 3.

Neil Spiller is Professor of Architecture and Digital Theory and Vice Dean at the Bartlett School of Architecture, University College London.

FREEZE

A Celebration of Design in the Modern North

Brian Carter reports from Anchorage, in Alaska, where he co-curated an art and architectural event in early 2009 that set out to celebrate the climate, landscape and light of the icy north.

Visitors enjoy a bonfire at the centre of molo's labyrinth.

FREEZE, an event held in Anchorage, Alaska, at the opening of 2009, was aptly named. Its aim was to bring together architects, artists and designers from across the world to explore ice, snow and light in a series of installations on various sites on a landscaped parkway in the city. Provided with a modest budget, volunteers, tools, equipment, water, ice and snow, each of the 14 participating teams was invited to develop a collaborative design and to work together to build it. Work began on 1 January, and 10 days later a new collection of large-scale public art projects was opened to the public.

Prompted by the Anchorage Museum and inspired by the impending completion of the new museum building designed by David Chipperfield, FREEZE was co-curated by an artist and an architect. In some of the lowest temperatures on record, the teams battled sub-Arctic extremes. They became inventors, scientists and constructors as they worked together on site to develop proposals, some of which, due to the short days in Alaska at that time of year, took advantage of the limited natural light, and considered alternative sources of light and the impact of darkness.

Each of the teams, which included participants from Iceland, Europe, Canada and the US, approached the project with different ideas and expertise. One team, which included lighting designer Claudia Kappl who had worked in Sweden, embedded tiny LEDs in snow to create gigantic piles of brightly coloured snowballs. Another, Ana Rewakowicz and Kobayashi + Zedda Architects, marked out a network of paths across a vast snowfield with cones of ice. Using traffic beacons as moulds, the team fabricated 350 ice cones and, by embedding motion-sensitive lights within them, defined paths along which the light changed as people moved through the field.

Molo, a group of architects and designers from Vancouver, collaborated with sound artist Ethan Rose from Portland, Oregon, to create a more conspicuous space-making structure. This was defined as a spiral almost 30 metres (98 feet) in diameter and formed by high walls of compacted snow to define a route. The entrance was marked with a wall of cut logs. As each visitor entered the maze-like structure they collected a log and, on arriving at the large central space at the heart of the spiral, helped to build a blazing fire. The heat and flickering light of the fire provided a welcome focus on cold days, and specially written sound compositions made the place a unique spot in the city.

Other teams devised projects that explored the structural potential and light qualities of large blocks of ice. While two of the teams developed ideas that focused on ramped walkways defined by snow walls, some with colour embedded within them, the project by Mayer Sattler-Smith and Marisa Favretto consisted of a large, freestanding

above left: LED lights by Sylvania create inner light for a thousand hand-constructed snowballs as part of Claudia Kappl's Snowball Effect installation.

above right: In Ana Rewakowicz and Kobayashi + Zedda Architects' Ice Fracture installation, motion-activated lights create a participatory experience at the edge of Anchorage's Delaney Park Strip.

right: A view from above the snow labyrinth of molo's Northern Sky Circle project.

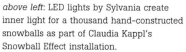

In its efforts to assemble teams of emerging designers from around the world, to encourage collaborative work and prompt new considerations of snow, ice and light in the north, FREEZE was a surprising and very successful public event, the impermanence of the work highlighting the ephemeral qualities of weather, the uncontrollability of nature and the potential of materials.

wall sited within a visual corridor that connected the city with the spectacular mountain range that defines Anchorage. Created by assembling large blocks of ice, this single battered wall with a carved-out circular disc on one face was fronted by a set of ice stairs. It successfully engaged the city grid and the extraordinarily beautiful and vast mountain range, and at the same time the stark, simple structure seemed to radiate light from the large icy-blue blocks from which it was made.

Other projects sought to project ideas about oil and water. CK Architecture and Lita Albuquerque from Los Angeles created a gigantic table across the landscape, the top of which was a tray of oil supported by a base of ice, and another project took the form of a pond that contained two cars frozen in the ice. Another defined a site by locating ancient icebergs from Anchorage harbour marked with layers that represented annual freeze and thaw cycles like the layers of a tree.

While thousands of visitors walked, crawled and skied through the installations, within a week of the public opening the temperature shifted and FREEZE began to thaw. Snow changed colour, ice became transparent and constructions melted away. In its efforts to assemble teams of emerging designers from around the world, to encourage collaborative work and prompt new considerations of snow, ice and light in the north, FREEZE was a surprising and very successful public event, the impermanence of the work highlighting the ephemeral qualities of weather, the uncontrollability of nature and the potential of materials. ⚙+

Brian Carter is an architect who worked in practice with Arup in London prior to taking up an academic appointment in North America. The curator of exhibitions on the work of Peter Rice, Albert Kahn and Eero Saarinen, he is also the author of numerous books. He is currently Professor and Dean of the School of Architecture & Planning at the University at Buffalo, The State University of New York.

Visitors gather at one end of CK Architecture and Lita Albuquerque's 30-metre (99-foot) Oil and Water Table constructed of snow and ice.

Architectural Design **Energies** May/June 2009

What is Architectural Design?

Launched in 1930, *Architectural Design* is an influential and prestigious architectural publication. With an almost unrivalled reputation worldwide, it is consistently at the forefront of cultural thought and design.

Architectural Design is published bimonthly. Features include:

Main section
The main section of every issue functions as a book and is guest-edited by a leading international expert in the field.

△+
The △+ magazine section at the back of every issue includes ongoing series and regular columns.

Truly international in terms of the subjects covered and its contributors, *Architectural Design*:

- focuses on cutting-edge design
- combines the currency and topicality of a newsstand journal with the rigour and production qualities of a book
- is provocative and inspirational, inspiring theoretical, creative and technological advances
- questions the outcomes of technical innovations as well as the far-reaching social, cultural and environmental challenges that present themselves today

How to Subscribe

With 6 issues a year, you can subscribe to △ (either print or online), or buy titles individually.

Subscribe today to receive 6 issues delivered direct to your door!

£198 / US$369   institutional subscription (combined print and online)

£180 / US$335   institutional subscription (print or online)

£110 / US$170   personal rate subscription (print only)

£70 / US$110   student rate subscription (print only)

To subscribe: Tel: +44 (0) 843 828
Email: cs-journals@wiley.com

To purchase individual titles go to:
www.wiley.com

Erratum
In the March/April 2009 issue, the article 'Automated Assessment of Early Concept Designs' was reported as authored by Chuck Eastman. In fact it was co-authored by Chuck Eastman, Jin-kook Lee, Hugo Sheward, Paola Sanguinetti, Yeon-suk Jeong, Jaemin Lee and Sherif Abdelmohsen.